I'M NOT DONE

I'M NOT

IT'S TIME TO TALK ABOUT
AGEISM IN THE WORKPLACE

DONE

PATTI TEMPLE ROCKS

LIONCREST
PUBLISHING

I'M NOT DONE

It's Time to Talk About Ageism in the Workplace

ISBN   978-1-5445-1374-4   *Hardcover*

978-1-5445-1238-9   *Paperback*

978-1-5445-1239-6   *Ebook*

This book is dedicated to all the "anonymous" people who shared their stories, to all those who feel compelled to stand up and say #ImNotDone, and to the strong, smart, and compassionate business leaders who are ready to listen and change.

And, of course, this book is also dedicated to my soul-nurturing family, especially my husband, Bob, and my son, Jake—neither of whom have ever believed for a moment that I am done.

CONTENTS

ACKNOWLEDGMENTS

I STARTED THINKING ABOUT THE TOPIC OF AGEISM in the workplace a decade ago, long before I decided to write this book. As I reflect back on my journey to this point, I am reminded of conversations I had when a book wasn't even a thought in my mind, yet somehow what was said in these conversations stuck with me and guided my pen to the page. So, my first thank-you goes to everyone who's been a part of those conversations, because you helped me open my eyes and my ears.

We should all be so lucky to have a mentor and a friend like Julie Fasone Holder. She has been there for me with each step I've taken in my career and life. Her advice and support have sustained me through it all. I didn't just listen to what she said, I watched what she did. And oh, how I learned.

Jan Fields: in addition to giving me one of my favorite lines ever, you also offered encouragement and sage advice, not just about this book, but about my life and my career.

I cannot emphasize enough how grateful I am to the people who shared their stories with me. These are often not very happy stories, and sometimes they hurt to talk about. I promised that I would not use their real names, which was their choice, but now I am pained that I can't name them here to publicly thank them. Angelina, William, Diana, Mary Lou, Brian, Emma, Nancy, and Alice, please know that without your stories, and your generosity in sharing them, there is no book.

Thank you for sharing examples of how to create a workplace free of ageist attitudes and biases. Tony Cortese, you and your colleagues at Herman Miller were an inspiration to me and I know will be to the readers as well; Susan Credle, thank you for believing (and saying out loud) that creativity has no expiration date; and Damaris and Jackie—you just keep doing what you're doing!

I cared very much about accuracy regarding the legal, human resources, and financial issues that impact the issue of ageism, and I am deeply grateful to Sue Ellen, Pamela, Mike, Nancy, Brian, and Sarah for specific guidance. We should all be grateful to AARP, the Society for

Human Resources, and the EEOC for continuing to research and track statistics about older workers. And to Elizabeth: "mature" job-seekers everywhere will appreciate your advice.

This is my first book, and I knew next to nothing about how to make that happen. I am grateful to my oh-so-talented team: Meghan, who edited with an expert's touch and a good person's heart; Erin, who designed a cover that is as direct and to-the-point as I am; Julie, who made sure all this happened on time, and coached a "newbie" through the process; and to Kelly, who will help make sure people read it!

To the instructors at SoulCycle, who may wonder if we are listening as we pedal...we are! Thank you to instructors all across the country for inspiring me to make change in my life, but especially to my OLTN homies, Brent, Aya, and Jaclyn. And to Amy, for telling me about SoulCycle; and Carrie, for going with me that first, scary time.

Thank you to my bosses, my clients, and my colleagues for the last four decades. You are my work tribe, and I have learned so much from you! Among the most important lessons I have learned is that caring about the people you work with is the first and most important step toward creating meaningful change. Thank you for caring about me and for letting me care about you. You give me optimism that we can and will address ageism.

Thank you, Fred, for truly hearing me when I needed to be heard.

To the family who surrounded me with love and a "you've got this" and "hell no you're not done" spirit, saying "thank you" doesn't seem like quite enough. To my husband Bob, who didn't freak out when I left my job; my son Jake, who may tell me I am a nerd but tells his friends I am a badass; my step kids Eric and Danielle for inviting me into their lives; my mom Nancy, who unconditionally supports me and my brother Pete (fellow first-time author!) who has been walking through this with me as he does with everything; my sister-in-law and chief cheerleader, Paige; and to my niece Mady and nephew Pace, who just always make me feel so loved and so cool, I will say not just thank you, but I love you.

And finally, to my grandfather, Robert Lindquist, who wrote his book in 1956 and inscribed my prized copy with the message "to my dear granddaughter and fellow writer, with much promise for the future." Though he died in the 1980s, he was with me for every word...and Grandpa, today, I am truly a writer.

I'm Blessed. I'm Grateful. *I'm Not Done.*

INTRODUCTION

WHEN IT COMES TO DISCRIMINATION IN THE WORK-place, we've come a long way as a society.

Gone are the days when staffing decisions were made based on race, gender, or other now-protected classes; while we've still got distance to travel on the road to true equality, we're currently enjoying a much more inclusive world than the one our parents lived and worked in. As such, while I knew discrimination was still an issue to be aware of, it wasn't at the front of my mind as a well-educated, successful professional in the 21st century.

So, when suddenly I found several of my friends and col-leagues—and then, alarmingly, myself—being pushed to the side at work, I was thrown for a loop.

About a decade ago, a dear friend of mine, Angelina, who was in her early 50s at the time, persuaded me to come back to the large American company (without naming names, let's just say: you've heard of it, and it's included in the Dow Jones Industrial Average) where we'd first met as colleagues. Professionally, Angelina was on a roll; she had worked her way up from her beginning in sales and marketing to become the first woman to reach the vaunted executive wing at the company, and she oversaw the entirety of both HR and Public Affairs. She hired me to run Communications for the Public Affairs side. We immediately introduced a new corporate advertising campaign, and it succeeded beyond anyone's expectations. To all watching, we were both excelling at what we were doing—and my friend, especially, was boosting an already stellar professional reputation.

Which is why I was baffled when I started to notice hints that she was being marginalized. It was as though her stock was slowly dropping, and I couldn't discern any possible reason why it would.

Her ideas were being dismissed; her authority was called into question. I noticed that she wasn't at some of the meetings she used to be included in. The sense that she was being pushed to the side started as an uneasy feeling in my gut that I initially ignored, thinking I had to be over-reacting. Eventually, this gut feeling became a certainty, as more and more signs pointed to what, deep down, I *knew* was happening.

At a company event one night, I found myself in a conversation over drinks with the CEO—an opportunity I didn't take lightly. I decided to tell him about what I'd been seeing. I knew he was a huge fan of Angelina's—he put her in the job, after all—so I figured once I told him what was happening, he would help me fix it.

After I explained what I'd noticed, I asked him straight out: "What do you think I can I do to help her? I see her being pushed aside more and more, and it doesn't make any sense."

His answer shocked me. "Patti," he said, "don't you see how this could be good for you?"

Confused, and a little disturbed, I responded, "What do you mean?"

"Listen, Angelina has been in this business a long time. Maybe she's just tired, that's all."

At the time, I had yet to learn that *tired* is common code used to describe older workers in an ageist environment. What I knew for sure at the time, though, was that "tired" was absolutely the *last* word I, or anyone who knew her, would ever associate with Angelina, who was a force to be reckoned with—a total dynamo.

That job was the closest access I'd ever had to the CEO at the highest-level position I'd ever held. It was also the moment my bubble burst.

I started to see the same pattern crop up more and more in the workplace. An older employee, whose work was just as good as ever, would suddenly find themselves the main character in an odd story created by management—they were "tired", detached, "set in their ways", "not innovative", "static". I noticed a whole language of code that was used to suggest that these older workers' value was corroding with every extra year they spent in their roles.

This happened across the board, to men and women, to every class of minority, to workers at every level of the business. The only common characteristic was their age.

These older employees, due to their many years at the company, also often had the highest salaries of any of their coworkers. When they were pushed out, they were usually replaced by much younger workers at half the salary. It was clear that the decision was largely financial; what amazed me was that this phenomenon wasn't just tolerated, it was widespread across industries. Baseless discrimination against an entire class of people had become a regular business practice.

My immediate reaction was resolute and determined: *I'll be damned if I let this happen to me.*

And then, of course, it happened to me.

WE WEREN'T DONE

Angelina's career at the company we both worked for ended with an appropriately respectful retirement package—but it was offered to her earlier than expected. It was made to seem like a compliment, but the message was clear: it was time for her to move on, and should she refuse the retirement package and stay at the company, she'd likely be sidelined more and more. That was not how she wanted to end her career.

By no means was Angelina *done* with her career, though. She went on to ramp up a busy consulting schedule, was offered seats on two different boards of directors for major blue-chip companies, and taught classes at the university level in her spare time. To say that she was "tired" wasn't just ludicrous, it was a lie, a convenient narrative that made it easy to get her to leave.

It feels funny even describing people like myself and

Angelina, and others our age, as "older workers", because I certainly don't *feel* old, and I'm sure Angelina would agree. There's a whole landscape of common stereotypes about people over the age of 50—that they're incapable of understanding tech, oblivious to news and trends, and unwilling to learn anything new—that I always scoffed at, because it seemed so off-base with me and others in my generation.

What's more, the narrative that, at some point, you will be expected to give up your career and "start your next chapter"—whatever *that* means—is well-supported throughout popular culture and media. There is an entire genre of self-help books out there aimed specifically at people my age, all about "finding your second-act career".

Here's my question: *why would I want a second-act career?*

I like my career. I do work that I love, and I'm great at it. I spent nearly four decades building expertise in an industry where expertise is the difference between success and failure. Why on earth would I want to leave it all behind to go open, say, a home jewelry business? I just might do that, but because it's my *hobby,* not my *career.*

I prepared myself for the inevitable squeezing out of my own presence and value at work; I figured that if I could recognize the signals, I'd be able to do something about it while it was happening.

The problem with this, I soon discovered, is that, when it *does* happen to you, when you're suddenly on the receiving end of the putting-out-to-pasture that myself and so many people I know experienced, quite often, *there are no signals.*

For me, there was certainly no warning whatsoever. I was at the top of my game at work; I was happy, I was engaged, I was well-regarded and well-respected. My reviews and results were positive. There was no signal that I was about to be pushed aside. And when it happened, my prevailing thought was: *I'm not done!*

Why should I have to end my career in any other way than exactly when and how I want to?

Why should *anyone?*

That overwhelming feeling—*I'm not done*—is the reason I wrote this book. I don't want to shuffle offstage and start my "second career". I don't want to write another book validating the view that a person's value as a professional only extends to a certain arbitrary age by suggesting that they plan for their "second act".

No one should ever have to feel sidelined or undervalued. I think there's a better way. In fact, I *know* there is. And it starts with having an open discussion about ageism.

I want to expose that despite all the progress we've made as a society toward a more inclusive, equal-opportunity work environment, we're still loath to include *age* in the discrimination conversation. We're currently experiencing an unprecedented longevity boom; baby boomers now represent 50% of the population and are living longer and staying healthier than any previous generation. As a result, the workers that are being pushed out of their careers early represent the single largest demographic currently living in the United States. That's a *lot* of institutional knowledge, a vast amount of professional experience and skill, that will be lost.

Even setting aside how ageism makes people feel (hint: *terrible*), most businesses are incredibly slow to realize—or totally blind to—the considerable upside of figuring out how to take advantage of this huge, highly capable segment of employees.

Ageism doesn't just hurt people; it hurts businesses, too. It's the last socially sanctioned prejudice. It's time to change that.

A RIDE AND A REALIZATION

About a year before I decided to write this book, I took a chance on the glowing recommendation of a friend and tried out a spin class at SoulCycle. She promised it would be as good for my soul as it was for my body. It wasn't something I had ever seen myself doing, but my knees had long since kept me away from running, and being out of shape was too depressing, so I decided to give it a go.

Five minutes in, I decided that my friend was *crazy*. I was exhausted and dripping with sweat, I couldn't figure out how to seat my shoes properly in the pedals, I couldn't understand the lingo being thrown around, and I was the oldest person in the room by far. If there were inspirational and soul-nurturing messages being voiced, I was either too tired or too confused to hear them.

I came back the next morning, though, and continued throwing myself into the 5:45 am class day after day. Something about that intimidating, overwhelming, loud, fast, work-focused environment made me feel a spark that felt downright awesome.

Pretty soon, I was able to put a name to that spark: I felt *empowered*.

And *empowered* was something I hadn't felt in a long time.

I'm someone who has always, throughout my life, plunged headfirst into challenge, and gone confidently in the direction of my dreams. I was the Managing Director of one of Chicago's biggest communications agencies. I worked on blue chip accounts. I was frequently asked to speak or serve on panels for industry events, and my advice and counsel were sought after by my staff and colleagues. I sit on the Board of Directors for a NASDAQ company. So why was I feeling like I had gotten to a place where I was no longer in control—where I felt sidelined, marginalized, and dismissed?

At work, I had recently been moved out of the influential, fulfilling role in which I was performing well and valued by my staff, and into what the business world might call an "independent contributor" role. But what it felt like to me was a role without much impact or influence. During a discussion I had with my boss about the situation, I made it clear that I wasn't happy with the new role, which didn't feel like a growth opportunity—or even a full-time position—to me.

After some back and forth, he asked, "Well, how much longer do you *really* want to work, anyway?" Ouch. I wasn't expecting that one, and boy did it sting.

That told me everything I needed to know about how I could hope to be perceived. After an incredibly successful and intense four-decade career, it had happened: I felt I had been devalued, right when I least expected it—when I believed I was at the very height of my skill and knowledge. And frankly, from the *last* company I ever expected it from. I truly loved that company, and had invested into it much more than my time—I'd invested my heart.

Do I think my boss, and my company, were being *intentionally* ageist? Honestly, no. That's my point, though: ageism isn't always intentional. My experience underscored just how hurtful, intentional or not, ageism can be. But much of the time, ageism is completely *unintentional*, and the result of systemic, unexamined, deep-seated beliefs that engender ageist behavior.

Throughout my career, when I looked around at the agency business, I could count on one hand the number of people who were my age, or even over the age of 50. Advertising and PR is not an industry that is friendly to older people; it's intensely youth-driven (some might even say *youth-obsessed*). I'd known this all along, because after all, I was an incredibly successful part of that industry. So in many ways, it didn't come as a surprise when, as an over-50 worker, I was the odd person out.

It took stepping into that SoulCycle studio every day to realize what I was no longer getting from my work, and how much I needed to make a change. When I sat on the bike, I didn't feel like the oldest person in the room. In fact, they have a sign that particularly inspired me. It looked exactly like the kind of sign you'd see in front of a roller coaster:

Ready to SOUL? To ride at SC you must be 4′11″ and 12 years old.

So essentially, the only requirements were that my feet reached the pedals and that I worked my ass off—and hard work has always come easily to me, so I excelled. At the same time, it highlighted that in my current role, that exhilarating feeling of knowing I was still "in it"—that I was making a meaningful difference—wasn't something I had felt in a while, or likely would feel again anytime soon. I was feeling anything *but* "in it" at work and had been feeling that way for a while. I hadn't realized how much it was affecting me emotionally, deep down, until I felt what it was to be empowered again.

I was able to make the choice that was right for me, and step away from the workplace that was marginalizing me. However, not everyone has that choice. Ageism is insidious, because not only does it rob people of the right to choose when they're ready to retire, it perpetuates a narrative that a person's value diminishes with every year they age; and should someone choose to continue on with their career, they will most certainly be made to *feel* that perceived loss of value. That emotional burden takes a serious toll.

Why have we decided to look the other way when our most experienced and capable employees and coworkers are made to feel less valued, even worthless—often for the first time ever, and at the end of what has otherwise been a great career?

BAD FOR PEOPLE, BAD FOR BUSINESS

"Everyone has a date stamped on their ass, and they're the only one who can't see it."

The first time I heard this, I assumed that it referred to other people at other companies. It couldn't *possibly* refer to the companies I'd poured so much of my time, effort, love, and passion into, right?

When I was proven wrong, it broke my heart. And I know I wasn't the only one at my company disillusioned and discouraged when I was pushed out; my younger colleagues watched it happen with a mix of confusion and apprehension. Their morale was also impacted, knowing that one day, they might expect the same treatment from the company to which they'd dedicated their working lives. I know this to be true, because I heard from them in large numbers, which was ultimately a big part of my motivation to write this book.

In these pages, you'll hear the stories of dozens of capable, high-performing professionals who were pushed out of their careers too early due to the subtle force of ageism. You'll learn the signs and signals that expose age discrimination within an organization. You'll see how that discrimination not only hurts people, but has a hugely detrimental effect on the operation, growth, and flourishing of a business by robbing that business of a valuable asset: capable, knowledgeable, and experienced workers.

You'll learn how what seems like a good financial choice—replacing high salaries with lower ones—actually costs a business far more down the road due to lost institutional memory and eroded morale.

You'll understand the legal side of the equation; age discrimination, after all, isn't legal, and your business could currently be exposed to a high degree of liability without you being aware of it at all.

You'll see the specific steps you can take to hold a mirror up to your own business and see if ageism is taking its toll on your people, and on your bottom line.

Even better, by the time you finish this book, you'll be

equipped to create a plan to eradicate ageism within your business, and reap the benefits of a truly inclusive, diverse workforce.

A BETTER WAY

My goal with this book is twofold:

One, I want to start an open conversation about ageism in the workplace. Nothing can change until we as a society own up to what's happening, decide to acknowledge it, and most importantly—*talk* about it.

Age discrimination is pervasive, but it's also subtle. It can be difficult to put your finger on, and it can be easy to feel like you're overreacting when you notice something that feels off. It's critical that we all begin to understand what ageism looks like, how it affects people at every level in a business, and how we can begin to unravel the common behaviors that support it—and even safeguard against those behaviors.

Two, I want to show business owners, CEOs, and those in a decision-making seat at the top levels of every industry that *there is a better way*.

There was an old joke at one of the big companies I used to work for (you'll forgive me, again, for not naming names):

What do you call someone over the age of 55 at Big Company?

CEO.

It doesn't have to be like this! It doesn't have to be "CEO or bust" for those over the age of 50. The younger employees don't have to look to their advancing years with the dread of knowing they'll eventually be put out to pasture, too. There's a better way, and in this book, you'll learn exactly how to make it happen within your organization.

It's time to give glorious careers the glorious, rather than *inglorious*, ends they deserve. It's time to get rid of the last acceptable form of discrimination and build our workplaces into the truly inclusive, diverse landscapes of experience the last few decades of progress have promised.

It's time to talk about ageism in the workplace!

CHAPTER ONE

THE NEW AGE OF AGING

"EVERYONE HAS A DATE STAMPED ON THEIR ASS, and they're the only one who can't see it."

This is from my friend Jan Fields, who gave the now famous quote to Fortune magazine in her response to her firing from her job. Jan's career and life story would be a great book in and of itself, but what struck me in the context of writing my own book was that Jan, who was 57 at the time of her firing, was a total spitfire who through hard work, dedication, and talent had risen to the pinnacle of corporate success.

And was promptly asked to retire.

The reason I love Jan's story (and Jan herself!) so much is because she is a born fighter. When she was pushed out, she refused to go quietly. Above all, she refused to let a false narrative become the official record of what happened. It would have been so easy to believe she had simply retired; she was technically old enough, and she certainly could afford to retire. Congratulations cards would have flooded her mailbox and no one would have thought twice about it.

But Jan told her company that she *would not* retire, that she wasn't ready to retire, and that if they wanted her to go, they would have to fire her.

So they did, and it was big news.

Pattie Sellers, from Fortune Magazine and the curator of Fortune's Most Powerful Women List (on which Jan was #25) called to ask her what had happened, and Jan decided to *tell it like it is*. This led to the above quote—my favorite quote ever.

Jan's story is similar to that of millions of men and women across the country. *She* wanted to be the one to decide when she retired. She embodies the new age of aging, and is most definitely #NotDone. Today Jan serves on the Board of Directors for Monsanto and Chico's, and is an in-demand public speaker.

I interviewed many victims of ageism for this book. Their stories all have certain similarities, and in their own way, they are all heartbreaking. You'll hear many of them in the coming chapters. But to fully comprehend the devastating effect of ageism, we must first understand the demographic group currently feeling its effects.

BABY BOOMERS THINK DIFFERENTLY

When Jan refused to retire, I was not surprised. Jan is a baby boomer, as am I. The baby boomers are the largest generation we've ever had in this country. Born between the 1940s and the 1960s, baby boomers are now in their fifties and sixties.

Baby boomers think differently. We are living longer, stronger, and healthier than any previous generation. To the generation before us, age fifty-five was considered "approaching retirement." But for Boomers, rapid advancements in medicine, health, nutrition, diagnostics, exercise, and diet have dramatically lengthened the average lifespan in this country.

We take our health seriously; I attend SoulCycle four days a week, and all my friends work out, lift weights, exercise, and eat right. We're not chasing the fountain of youth for vanity's sake; we just don't see any reason to stop behaving this way. The fitness industry happily accommodates us. Some marathons have even added categories for runners over the age of seventy! And why wouldn't they? Just imagine the lost revenue if the health and fitness industry bought into ageism!

FIFTY IS THE NEW FORTY

I believe in the notion that sixty is the new fifty, and fifty is the new forty. Who would ever consider retiring in their forties? It doesn't make sense, especially when we have so much more to give to our careers. We don't see ourselves as old in mind or body. And we believe our life lessons and career experience are priceless.

As Boomers, we have a lot to give, and *so* much more to do. There are so many stories of Boomers who went back to college or graduate school after age fifty; people in their fifties are going to law school, and millions of them are starting businesses. Boomers are the first generation in which millions of women are the primary breadwinners in their households, so the notion that the woman's income is "fun money" is as antiquated as it is offensive.

According to Peter Hubbell, author of *The Old Rush: Marketing for Gold in the Age of Aging,* baby boomers are not trying to age gracefully—they are *redefining aging entirely.* Hubbell writes:

The Boomers have always been ambitious dreamers, and more often than not, they have achieved that which they have conceived. As their lives have proceeded, their dreams have become ever more vivid, almost as if they are daring themselves to prove they still have what it takes to be great. Dreams? Perhaps, but they sure do seem pretty real. This generation is just getting started with their next act in their lives and it's going to be a fascinating show.

It's not a surprise that remaining in the workforce is what millions of baby boomers want. They intend to keep working. They take pride in their work and in their careers. They dislike the idea of retiring; they want to continue contributing to society.

Above all, they absolutely do not want to be told by someone else when it's their time to retire; they want to be in control of their careers and lives. In other words, *please don't cut us out!* Don't underestimate us. Don't sideline us, or otherwise diminish what we've got left.

Many of the most successful and influential people in the world are way older than fifty or sixty. Pope Francis is in his eighties; Supreme Court justice Ruth Bader Ginsburg is eighty-five. Warren Buffett is eighty-eight. Many US Senators are in their seventies and eighties, and they show no signs of slowing down or retiring.

A recent study titled *the 2017 Retirement Confidence Survey* polled different age groups about when they expect to retire. Thirty-five percent of Millennials surveyed said they think they're going to retire before age sixty-five. In contrast, only nineteen percent of baby boomers said they think they'll retire before sixty-five. And get this, fifteen percent of boomers actually said they don't think they're ever going to retire.

Plus, many boomers *need* to keep working. They have children in college and mortgages to pay. Social Security and Medicare don't kick in until age sixty-five. So how are boomers who retire at age fifty-five supposed to survive another decade with no income and no medical benefits?

Boomers have so much more to contribute to the workforce and to the economy. Unfortunately, they bear the brunt of ageism in our society. But as they've done so many times in the past, boomers are now willing to step up and say *no more*. Collectively as the boomer generation, *we're not done!*

FACTS ABOUT BABY BOOMERS

- Ages: 53-71

- Population: 74.3 M

- Nearly two-thirds of boomers expect to work past age 65

- Boomers make up over 41% of consumer spending and are twice as likely to be business owners than millennials

- By 2024, more than 40% of Americans over 55 will be employed, making up more than one-fourth of the U.S. workforce—the single largest age cohort

- The population of working adults who are 65 or older is expected to rise by 75% between now and 2050, compared to 2% growth for workers 25-64

- In the US, 10,000 people turn 65 every day

- Most people can expect to live thirty years post-retirement

- It is estimated that only 25% of Americans are prepared emotionally and financially for retirement

- The 60+ population is growing faster than any other

- By the year 2024, workers age 55+ will be the single largest demographic group in the workforce

WHAT *IS* AGEISM, EXACTLY?

One of the leading experts on this topic, Ashton Apple-white, is the author of *This Chair Rocks: A Manifesto Against Ageism.* Here is her definition:

Ageism occurs when the dominant group uses its power to oppress or exploit—or simply ignore—people who are much younger, or significantly older. We experience ageism any time someone assumes we're "too old" for something—a task, a relationship, a haircut—instead of finding out who we are and what we are capable of.

For reasons that don't make sense, ageism is the last socially acceptable "ism" in our society. Yet no one is organizing anti-ageism marches. Cable news generally doesn't report about highly-qualified professionals in their fifties who get marginalized and forced out of their jobs. Ageism is alive and well. Ageism shows no signs of stopping.

But why?

THE CAUSES OF AGEISM

There are many reasons ageism is so pervasive in our society. For one thing, unfair and unfounded stereotypes run rampant about workers over the age of fifty. *They can't master new skills. They don't understand technology. They're set in their ways. They're not open to new ideas. They're not creative. They can't handle stress. They have less energy than younger employees. They can't use an iPhone.* The list goes on and on.

Frankly, all of those stereotypes are absolute *nonsense*. Some of the most adaptable, tech-savvy, digitally sophisticated, and successful executives and entrepreneurs are over the age of fifty. Most Silicon Valley venture capitalists responsible for investing in the latest bleeding-edge technology startups are well into their sixties. If older workers were set in their ways, didn't understand technology, and weren't open to new ideas, then the VC world would be run by millennials. It's not! It was the wisdom and experience of the boomers in the VC world that led to saying "yes" to some truly great ideas.

Here's another example. One stereotype I heard a lot in the agency business is that older employees can't relate to younger consumers and millennials. On the contrary, most people in their fifties know the millennial mindset extremely well, because they have children who are millennials. I'm way better at understanding millennials than someone who is thirty or forty years old, because as a stepmom to two kids now in their 30s, and mom to a 22-year-old, I've had a house full of millennials for the past twenty years. Talk about a built-in focus group— all of my kids, as well as their friends, have helped me workshop many a new business pitch! I would argue that's something older workers bring to the workplace: an understanding of the millennial demographic group that comes from raising them in our own homes.

Besides stereotypes, another cause of ageism is financial. Workers who have been with the same company for decades tend to earn significantly higher salaries than new hires in their twenties and thirties. That's as it should be. All of those years of experience have tremendous value to an organization.

But older workers who are earning twice as much as workers half their age may start to feel like they have a target on their back. Most organizations resent when older employees are highly paid but don't deliver enough value to justify their salary. Sadly, most companies don't know how to deal with this. So they decide to force the older employee out, make them take a retirement package offer, or reassign them to a difficult job they'll be miserable in until they decide on their own to quit.

A much better path forward is to have an honest conversation with the employee, state the company's concerns openly, and work together to come to possible solutions.

This won't come as a surprise, but almost all of the people I interviewed for this book felt they were pushed out because they were earning a high salary. However, this might surprise you: many of the people had awareness, even understanding, of that business and financial reality. One person told me, "If someone would have come to me and told me their concern, I gladly would have had a conversation about it. I wish I knew there were options other than being fired."

There *are* other options.

Perhaps an employee could take a reduced role at a reduced salary with full benefits. Maybe they could go part-time, or work as an independent consultant, or even take on additional responsibilities in order to justify their advanced salary. There are options, but not a lot of proven examples of what works, because unfortunately, most companies aren't having these honest conversations with older workers. It's probably because having the end-of-career conversation is painfully awkward, so most companies just don't do it.

Another reason older people are discriminated against is the idea that investing in younger employees will yield a higher return over the long term. The thinking goes like this: *Why should we spend money on training for Paul, who's in his mid-fifties? He'll only be around a few more years. But if we invest in Rachel, who's in her thirties, we'll earn an ROI on that investment for another twenty-five years.*

Maybe I'm alone on this, but if I've got a long road trip ahead of me, given a choice between a Mercedes S-Class with 100,000 miles on it and a brand-new Chevy Cruze... my choice is *definitely* the luxury vehicle, no matter how many miles it has.

"Younger and cheaper is better" certainly sounds logical, but it's a fallacy. Workers over the age of fifty generally aren't out looking for another job. They're not job-hopping. In contrast, millennials are unlikely to spend their entire careers at a single company. They're most likely going to take that investment you made in them and take it to another company for a higher salary. So contrary to popular belief, it *does* make more sense to invest in older workers who are likely to remain loyal employees for years to come.

There are also cultural reasons for age discrimination. Just watch the late-night talk shows any night and you'll hear plenty of jokes poking fun at older people. Watch sitcoms, network TV shows, movies, and even cartoons; age jokes are a comedy staple. Older people are routinely portrayed as decrepit, out of touch, or forgetful. Terms like "old-timer," "Granny," and "Grandpa" are said in a derogatory and unflattering tone. Walk into any drugstore and browse the greeting card aisle; you'll see cards implying that people age forty are "over the hill". Fiftieth birthday cards usually depict rocking chairs and old-age gag gifts. And if you happen to watch Fox News, you can't help but assume that everyone over 50 needs walkers, erectile dysfunction drugs, and a cell phone with an emergency button!

The cumulative result is a growing lack of respect of

people over fifty that has become pervasive. It's almost become acceptable to treat anyone over fifty like they should be in a retirement home. Media and entertainment have fostered a culture where it's okay to make fun of older people.

As if older workers don't already have it bad enough, it doesn't help when one of the most influential people on the planet reinforces the stereotype that older workers are inferior to younger ones. According to *VentureBeat*, Mark Zuckerberg, founder of Facebook, said at a tech conference, "Young people are just smarter."

Wow. Really, Mark? It's not surprising that Facebook was later sued by an older worker who claims he was discriminated against on the basis of age.

Older Americans have power. We are a formidable group. Just look at our spending power: by one estimate, older Americans control $2.6 trillion in annual spending. That's substantially more than the $2.26 trillion of millennials. But for some reason, advertisers covet the millennial market, and almost shun the older demographics.

Ageism really is an accepted form of discrimination. When someone forgets something, or makes a mistake, you might hear someone say, "That was a senior moment." But as a society, we would never accept someone saying, "That was a *Hispanic* moment." Or, "That was an *Asian* moment." For some reason, when it comes to age, anything goes. There is no stigma conferred upon jokes or slurs that denigrate older people.

That needs to change.

> ## THINK ABOUT THE END OF YOUR CAREER, NOT JUST THE BEGINNING
>
> Almost all of the ambitious young people I meet spend a lot of time thinking and talking about the early stages of their career. They put a lot of energy into getting the right internships, finding their first job, and then earning a promotion. I did the same thing, but what I now know is that none of them give a single thought to managing the tail end of their career.
>
> That's a shame, because navigating the last ten years of a career can be even more difficult than the first ten. The stakes are certainly higher. When you're young, you have plenty of time to course correct if you make a mistake that detours your career. But when you're fifty-five, if you aren't paying attention to your career and end up in a non-essential job, that can be career ending. It pays to have a strategy.

THE BENEFITS OF AGE DIVERSITY

We hear about the benefits of diversity all the time. But usually, this refers to diversity of ethnicity, culture, country of origin, religion, and so on. Rarely have I heard anyone mention diversity of age.

I think real magic happens when organizations make a

concerted effort to incorporate age into their diversity initiatives. When a team is made up of younger "digital natives" who grew up on the internet and social media, along with more senior employees who have decades of industry experience, there is a synergy of talents and abilities. Everyone learns from one another. That combination of wisdom, experience, and youth is powerful.

I also believe that every business is more successful when they have employees who represent the population at large. If the population is getting older, your workplace should be getting older, too. If an organization is underrepresented by people in their 50s and 60s, then guess what? That organization no longer mirrors the population.

BOOMERS IN THE WORKPLACE

Despite rampant ageism, there are more older Americans in the workplace than ever before. And they're accomplishing more than any generation before them. Because older workers are staying in their careers longer, a new paradigm is emerging. Here are seven key trends that I see in the new baby boomer mindset.

THE WISE BOOMER

Wisdom matters. Boomers don't see themselves as old, in either mind or body. They want to be recognized and appreciated for the knowledge and skills they've gained over a lifetime. They want to contribute in a meaningful way, including the ability to pass along their wisdom and life experience.

SIXTY IS (REALLY) THE NEW FIFTY

Boomers are intent on re-inventing aging in their own fun-loving image. Boomers are going back to school, launching businesses, running marathons. They don't know the concept of "age-appropriate," and they still feel great.

THE "I GOT THIS" ATTITUDE

Long defined by their independent, trailblazing approach to life, boomers are resistant to receiving support that threatens their autonomy. Their millennial children don't always understand this.

WHAT RETIREMENT?

Boomers look at retirement completely differently from previous generations. The old cliché of retirement meaning an end to all work is fading away. Boomers like having an impact in every way they can, and will be as creative as they need to be in finding opportunities.

NO MOVING TRUCK REQUIRED

Not all boomers become snowbirds. Many are choosing to stay closer to home to remain connected to others—particularly their children and grandchildren. Some are even opting to move into their children's neighborhoods so they can stay active in their grandchildren's lives. Plus, they're totally comfortable jumping on a plane and finding an Airbnb when they crave a little sunshine.

CONSTANTLY CONNECTED

Boomers are readily adopting technology and using social media just as much as younger generations do. In fact, they are much more likely to share, advocate, and influence others online.

PROUD...JUST NOT ALWAYS OUT LOUD

While boomers are often justifiably proud of how young they look, feel and act, sometimes that results in an effort, conscious or otherwise, to disguise their actual age. Many go so far as to dye their hair, hide their age, and fudge how old they really are—all to appear younger in their place of work. Even worse, sometimes older people appear to discriminate against themselves by not being more aggressive in calling out ageism when they see it.

I believe that to be a mistake. We should all embrace our age, and the experience and wisdom that comes with it.

Despite all these positive attributes of boomers, employers still don't seem to be able to eradicate ageism from the workplace. For the past couple of decades, companies have been bombarded with information about how to deal with younger generations in the workplace. But rarely does that information address older generations.

There is now an unlimited number of seminars and workshops on how to tailor the workplace to meet the needs of up and coming generations. We've been taught how to recruit them, how to train them, and how to engage them so that they stay in the workplace.

Sadly, all this focus on the under-forty crowd has had an unintended consequence for the workforce: a devalued older workforce, which has resulted in rising age discrimination claims by older workers. We'll talk more about why in the coming chapters.

———

CHAPTER TWO

BAD FOR PEOPLE, BAD FOR BUSINESS

I'VE SEEN FIRSTHAND HOW AGEISM AFFECTS people on a personal level, as a practice that is harmful because of how it perpetuates a dangerous corporate behavior pattern that demotivates, discourages, and disrespects people at all levels of an organization.

Put simply, ageism is bad for people because it marginalizes and hurts them.

I'd like to think that alone is a reason to change. But business is business, and people aren't the only ones hurt by ageism. Ageism represents a very real financial threat to businesses, and any business leader should be aware of the risks posed by age discrimination if left unchecked.

THE LEGAL DEFINITION

According to the US Equal Employment Opportunity Commission (EEOC), age discrimination is defined as follows:[1]

> Age discrimination involves treating an applicant or employee less favorably because of his or her age. The Age Discrimination in Employment Act (ADEA) forbids age discrimination against people who are age 40 or older.

The ADEA was created in 1967 and prohibits age discrimination in any "aspect of employment, which can include hiring, firing, pay, job assignments, promotions, layoffs, training, benefits, and any other term or condition of employment."

So, it's not just hiring and firing that a business should be concerned about when it comes to ageism—it's essentially *all* aspects of work, down to the very types of assignments given to employees. I hope you noted that the protected class starts at 40—and you likely have employees in your organization who can, and want to, work well into their 60s or 70s.

THE TALENT POOL

It's said that some businesses—like advertising agencies,

---

1   https://www.eeoc.gov/laws/types/age.cfm

for one—are "a young person's game". The communications industry in general suffers from an obsession with youth that robs it of the ability to resonate across a diverse audience. This isn't just a cliché, nor is it just a problem in the US; the Institute for Practitioners in Advertising, a UK group, confirms that the average age of employees at all IPA member agencies is 33.7, a figure that has remained static since 2009. It skews a little older in the US, where the average age is all of 38.

In the agency business, in many businesses for that matter, it's all about talent. In fact, it's often an all-out war for talent. Given this, a natural question that any business leader in a youth-driven industry should be asking themselves is: *How can we possibly afford to let ageism drive good talent out?*

I recently saw an interview with a former Chief Creative Officer of a major London advertising agency (name withheld). Here's what he had to say:

> The industry is in danger of becoming a zero-sum game. For most of us, it has become about numbers and margins, and *people* are reduced to a statistic. When you cut 30% of an agency's overhead or cut the highest earners ahead of a potential sale, this disproportionately affects older staff.

Another industry that has earned a high degree of negative attention on the issue of worker age is the tech industry. The stereotype that older workers are set in their ways, non-tech-savvy, non-digital-natives is what's at play here; youth is seen as the gateway to technological innovation, adaptation, and expertise. As a result, the tech industry has seen some of the most blatant ageism on the map, especially when it comes to hiring practices. It's no surprise, then, that tech companies are currently experiencing a talent shortage that has driven salaries higher and reduced the overall agility of the organization.

In 2016, the median age of a Facebook employee was 29; at Google, 30; at Apple, 31. In the same year, HP, Oracle, and IBM all had workforces with a median age between 35 and 40.

Consider the privacy scandal Facebook has been dealing with since 2017. If the median age of their employees is 29, how many people at the company truly have the experience to address such a massive public relations disaster? That kind of skill and expertise only comes with on-the-job time spent handling company-wide disasters and navigating public opinion—it's not something you learn in college, in company onboarding, or in a crisis management summit.

Failing to have a plan to attract, retain, and engage older workers could cause you critical staff shortages. The problem could be especially bad for small and medium-sized businesses that aim to retain older workers; especially in creative industries, younger staff are missing the invaluable mentoring that only experienced older colleagues can provide.

It cannot be overstated: failing to address age discrimination within your business leaves your company open to massive financial and legal risk. It's not a matter of *if* the company will get sued; with the number of baby boomers nearing retirement age swelling year after year, it's a matter of *when.* I'll discuss this in more detail in Chapter Four.

Tech companies, seeking workforces that skew young, intentionally screen out older candidates before they can even be considered for a job. This has resulted in increased legal exposure, and indeed, at the time of this writing, both Google and Facebook are currently named in lawsuits due to their alleged discriminatory hiring practices.

THE CULTURE HIT

With *culture* a corporate buzzword these days, and businesses hiring expensive outside consultants to show them how to build the kind of coveted, exemplary company culture that attracts the best talent and allows them to scale, it's baffling that so few business leaders understand how drastic a hit ageism can be to those very efforts.

The difference between ageism and other forms of discrimination is that everyone—unless they're unlucky, and a tragedy befalls them—gets old. *Everyone* within a company is subject to the possibility of falling victim to ageism. It's a lot harder to look the other way, think, *well, at least that won't happen to me,* or be safe within any kind of privilege bubble when you know it's only a matter of time before you're in the same boat as the coworker who was just marginalized and pushed out due to their age.

When you're thirty-five and working hard toward the peak achievement years of your career, it's terribly demoralizing to watch a fifty-five-year-old colleague be diminished with ageist rhetoric. It's all too easy to imagine it happening to you, too.

What kind of environment does this create? How productive—and how *loyal*—can any employee be expected to be when they're fully and painfully aware of the limited extent of their value to the organization?

A strong company culture can't flourish when employees are shown evidence that they're disposable.

VALUABLE TO THE END

There was a time—and this thinking still exists in some larger companies, although it's generally waning—when workers of a certain age felt justified in coasting through the rest of their tenure. If that's true in your organization, while not a negative result of ageism, it needs to be rectified just the same. No matter your age, you *have* to be good at what you do and valuable to your organization if you want to be valued. I would abandon the #ImNot-Done movement in a heartbeat if anyone perceived it as protectionism.

My message to older workers is this: never stop being good, and never stop trying to be better.

Ironically, ageist company cultures only *promote* the "senioritis" phenomenon. General disengagement is all too easy when a worker knows they're likely to be marginalized as they age. The above thought quickly becomes, *why bother giving it my all when they're just going to push me out anyway?*

Strong company culture reinforces pedal-to-the-metal engagement and productivity throughout the lifetime of a career. Ageism, in so many ways, subtly promotes easing off the gas, and it's the company's productivity that suffers as a result.

A GOOD CULTURE IS A DIVERSE CULTURE

The word "diversity" means "the state of being diverse; variety; a range of different things." "Diversity," the word, derives from the word "different," which is defined as "not the same as another or each other; unlike in nature, form, or quality; distinct; separate."

Simply put, diversity means any differentiation between a person, place, or thing. For our purposes, it specifically means "different people" or "people who are not the same."

Traditional determinations of "difference" stem from the Civil Rights era, and focus on external distinctions like race, ethnicity, and gender. These days, we also determine difference in new ways. Diversity thinking has expanded to include our experiences, our age, and our thoughts or views. We have even started to include aspects of our lives like the size of the city people are from, if they're from a red state or a blue state, and how they vote.

Put simply, we've realized that a fully inclusive look at the world and its population has to be expanded beyond the basics of our biographies.

This change did not occur as a result of an external force like the civil rights movement; rather, it came about due to the necessities of business itself. In order to keep up with the speed of technology, business leaders began to realize that diversity is a key foundation of innovation, a key ingredient of *success*. Nothing impedes success more than the groupthink and echo chambers that arise when everyone is alike and therefore *thinks* alike.

Ironically, though, age is still largely absent from the diversity conversation.

According to Price Waterhouse Cooper's 18th annual survey of CEOs, when asked how many of their diversity and inclusion strategies included a conversation around the issue of age, only 8% said it did. This means that even CEOs are realizing a lack of age diversity in their companies. In the same vein, the Society of Human Resources Professionals acknowledges that HR departments are not dealing with this issue either. While businesses have jumped on the #MeToo bandwagon and deserve credit for addressing gender inequality, they are still turning a blind eye to age discrimination. Even more ironically, remember this from earlier: ageism is the one "status" or affinity that ultimately affects us all. Everyone—no matter their sex, gender, race, experience, background, and ethnicity—gets old.

If, as we old folk often joke, "youth is wasted on the young," it is fair to say that age, wisdom, and experience are in danger of being wasted in many businesses. Diversity and inclusion might top the agenda—but an awareness of ageism is conspicuously absent.

To be crystal clear, when I talk about age diversity, I'm not just talking about older people here; businesses need twenty-year-olds as much as they need sixty-year-olds. Diversifying a business's workforce according to age is the right thing to do morally *and* economically. Diversity of thought simply cannot be achieved without age diversity.

According to Daniel Goleman, Author of *Emotional Intelligence:*

> High performing teams are dynamic and able to rise to the increasingly complex challenges of businesses today. But there's much more to this productivity than just technical skills. The interplay of perspectives can be vastly more important to a team's success than their hard skills. Vibrant teams where strengths are accentuated, and weaknesses compensated for, are those teams that are made up of very diverse people and have been trained to operate in an inclusionary way. A diverse team is one that is comprised of numerable experiences...innumerable experiences including age and experience. And it is also of course things like race, gender, and spirituality. These are the lenses through which we interpret the world, and these are the lenses that allow people to solve complex business problems.

At the end of the day, when it comes to building a great company culture, a mindset shift is necessary. Diversity is not a box to be checked, nor is it a *program*—it is a culture. Company culture needs to welcoming and inclusive to *all*. Older workers are not going away, and a business should set the example of valuing these older workers from the top down.

I often ask HR departments: how much are you talking about age when you conduct inclusivity workshops?

The answer is almost always "not much." These workshops almost always focus on racism, sexism, and better-known forms of discrimination—not ageism.

When I hear this, I then ask what's being done to change that. You can probably guess the answer I usually get— *not much!*

The problem is that ageism simply isn't on many CEO's agendas. Bottom line: senior leadership needs to send a signal to the entire organization that this is important.

WHAT THIS MEANS FOR YOUR BUSINESS

So, if the downsides to business are so huge, why do companies still engage in age discrimination, either intentionally or due to passive failure to stamp it out?

The plain truth is that there is a strong business proposition to squeezing out older workers, and it comes down to salary. I mentioned this concept before. By the time an employee has spent two or three decades at a company, they've likely been promoted to a level of salary that represents anywhere from two to *five* junior employees. If the company needs to make budget cuts, what's the natural choice? If you could get five workers for the price of one, wouldn't *you* cut the highest-paid older employee you have, and convert their salary into five new hires?

Rationalizing this decision would be relatively simple. *It's a business decision. It's not personal—it's a budget requirement. They're so close to retirement anyway, they'll probably be happy to stop working early. Her husband works, they don't need the money.* The list of rationalizations goes on and on.

And then the stereotypes that have been allowed to flourish in our culture pour in to further back up your rationalizing: *He's seemed tired lately anyway. How much innovation can I really expect from him? He's set in his ways. He doesn't understand new tech and new ideas—it's getting harder and harder to train him.*

It's a thought pattern that isn't just natural to follow, it's well supported by the structures of bias our society has put in place. It's all too easy to—even unintentionally—fall into ageist thinking.

It would be disingenuous *not* to acknowledge the financial realities that reinforce age discrimination. Payroll is far and away the highest expense for any business, and when it comes to competitive advantage in the market, the company that can grow the fastest will generally have that advantage—so it's not surprising that when cuts happen, it's to the highest salaries, usually held by those workers with the longest tenure.

I don't want to paint a picture of a mustache-twirling corporate exec cackling to himself while intentionally targeting the oldest employees on the payroll. Things aren't that cartoonish—unlike other forms of discrimination, rarely does someone have a deep-seated prejudice against older people. Because, again, *everyone gets old.*

When it comes to payroll cuts, ageist thinking doesn't usually *begin* the process. Rather, age discrimination is the natural result of cutting the highest salaries, and ageist thinking, reinforced by the accepted stereotypes rampant in our society, offers an easy route to rationalization. It lessens the blow on the decision-maker to be able to turn to nice-sounding explanations for their behavior. *Patti must be ready to slow down; she doesn't seem as involved in the business as she used to be. It's time to put her out to pasture. She'll probably be grateful. Who doesn't want to retire, anyway?*

My answer to that line of thinking is twofold: first, how do you know if you haven't asked me? And second, who is *anyone else* to decide when I'm done? I'll decide when I want to retire, thank you very much.

WHAT IS AND ISN'T AGE DISCRIMINATION

So, if you fire someone over the age of 40, is it automatically age discrimination at play?

The short answer is *no*. It's not automatically ageism. There are legitimate reasons to fire someone, no matter their age—if they're underperforming, for one, or if they commit offenses against the company like harassing other employees. Also, if the company faces the need for layoffs, it's only natural that some over-40 employees will be caught up in that resource action.

However, as a business leader, you should have a plan in place to ensure that such actions don't unevenly impact a single group. It's common that over-40 workers are disproportionately penalized when it comes time for layoffs; this is because layoffs often cut a slice through the higher-paying salaries at a company, and those higher-paying salaries are more commonly held by older, more experienced workers.

I can think of two recent examples. One was a large, global CPG (Consumer Packaged Goods) company who, in an effort to "flatten" the organization, decided to eliminate an entire level. But of course, they didn't choose a *junior* level (with lower salaries across the board): they chose a Director/VP level. As a result, the vast majority of the people impacted by that decision were in their 50s. Similarly, a colleague from a consulting company told me that when faced with an upcoming layoff, one of the managing partners asked his HR leader for a list of employees ranked by birth year. Yikes! Fortunately, the HR leader knew not to supply that list.

The irony here is that most companies rank "experience" as one of the most important qualifiers for any role. Look at any job ad; the base requirements will usually include anywhere from five to ten or more years of experience in a few specific disciplines, experience that it is completely impossible for most younger workers to have, because they simply haven't been in the workforce that long.

What's another line you'll almost always see in a job ad? *Pay commensurate with experience.*

So, companies desperately *want* experienced workers,

and are willing to pay for that experience. Yet when a company is financially challenged, that experience is the easiest target for a cost reduction.

This vicious circle isn't sustainable. It hurts people, and it hurts business.

CHAPTER THREE

THE MIRROR TEST

WHEN I BEGAN INTERVIEWING PEOPLE AND COL-
lecting information for this book, I tested my assumptions
every time. I would always start an interview by asking
people, "What do you think? Is ageism a thing? Is it real?"

The confirmation was as clear as it was definitive: ageism
is a thing. It's widespread. Unless all the people I talked
to were from another planet, business leaders today are
far more ageist than they think they are. But it also came
through loud and clear that these business leaders often
don't *realize* they are ageist.

It was discouraging to hear this, but I'm a glass-half-full
sort of person. I chose to believe that it's a good sign that
business leaders don't realize how ageist they are.

Here's why: discrimination, when it's malicious and intentional, can be a hard thing to solve. But I believe that discrimination against older workers is not purposeful or cruel but instead the result of unconscious bias. Employers don't comprehend the problem, but if we reveal the problem to them and convince them it's happening, they will change.

I'm optimistic for other reasons. Many employers will change once they're aware of their discrimination against older workers, but even more will change when they realize how important older workers are to the bottom line and the success of their business. This cohort of older, experienced, and emotionally intelligent workers is a tremendously valuable asset for business.

What's more, studies from ADP Research Institute, Moody's, the Bureau of Labor Statistics, and countless others show we're mired in a huge shortage of skilled workers.[2] When employers understand that problem, their attitude toward older workers is bound to change. They *need* these workers. Employers can't afford to cast them off or marginalize them. Business leaders need these older workers to continue doing what they've trained their whole adult lives to do.

But the first step is to hold a mirror up for employers so

---

2   https://www.adpemploymentreport.com/

they can see their unconscious bias against older workers. Does your company systematically push older workers out the door? Do you give all the new jobs to younger people? Do you cut older employees out of the bonus pool because you assume they'll be leaving soon anyway?

This is the mirror test and it requires honesty. If we can show employers how they discriminate, and they can see it and acknowledge that it's happening and that it's hurting their business, as someone who prefers my glass half full, I truly do believe they will change.

AN ACTION PLAN

The first thing we can do is change our language. How many times have you heard something described as a "senior moment"? Anything followed by "for her age" is demeaning. There are so many expressions like that. When people talk about our shifting demographics and how there will be a greater percentage of older people in the coming years, they call it a "gray tsunami". Tsunamis are a destructive and unfortunate event! Can't we come up with a more respectful word for that demographic phenomenon?

Experts call the use of these terms microaggressions. Microaggressions impact people by eroding self-esteem, causing psychological damage, and worst of all, closing doors to opportunities that should be open. All of these terms also reinforce the unconscious biases that people have. *You can't teach an old dog new tricks.* If you've heard that phrase a thousand times, you likely implicitly believe it's true, and that belief informs your actions.

If you want to find out if you or your company is ageist, here are some questions to ask and steps you can take.

HAVE YOU PERSONALLY ASKED YOUR WORKERS OVER FIFTY WHAT THEY EXPERIENCE AT YOUR COMPANY? WHAT ARE THEY FEELING?

Sarah is a senior human resources person for a large company, and among her many responsibilities, she helps people through the company's retirement process. She handles several each quarter. She told me that, time and again, an older worker will come to her, announce their plan to retire, but then go on to say things like, "I still feel really good. I still travel. I know I can still add value to the company but for some reason I'm just not feeling like I should stay here anymore. The business world seems to think it's time for me to stop. So, I guess I will." In other words, it's clear as day to Sarah that they're not really ready to retire.

When I asked Sarah if this was the result of ageism, she didn't hesitate: "Definitely," she said. "There is a significant percentage of people who not ready to retire who are retiring because they feel *pressure* to retire."

Does that sound like your company?

ARE YOUR TRAINING AND DEVELOPMENT OPPORTUNITIES DESIGNED AND DEVELOPED WITH ALL YOUR EMPLOYEES IN MIND?

If you're a manager and you're considering who to send to an upcoming training on some significant new technology—such as artificial intelligence—do you automatically think you should send the thirty-year-old instead of the fifty-year-old? You might reason that thirty-year-old Susie would make a better candidate. Susie might be with the company for a longer time than fifty-year-old Sam, and you will get a better return on your investment by sending Susie.

As such, you make a conscious decision to send Susie to the AI training. But four years down the road, you start thinking, *Sam hasn't kept up with technology as well as these younger employees. Maybe it's time for Sam to retire.* If you find yourself believing this, you have to think back and realize that you, as a manager, had an opportunity to help Sam keep his skills sharp and aligned with the changing needs of your company, and *you decided against doing that.*

Is it Sam's fault, then, that he hasn't kept pace? Not entirely; you have to take some responsibility for that. A truly "agenostic" approach would be to disregard an employee's age and decide instead on what's best for individuals and for the company on the basis of skill, experience, and talent.

The manager also failed to understand that older workers have a perspective about technology that younger workers don't have. Older employees remember when the internet was new and when social media in business was new; they have a sense of the big changes technology makes in business, and that perspective can help a company navigate changes in the future.

Can't teach an old dog new tricks? Perhaps the *manager* was the old dog in this scenario.

DOES YOUR EMPLOYEE HANDBOOK ADDRESS AGE DISCRIMINATION?

When I asked HR professionals about this, a *huge* number said, "Oh, my God. I don't think it does."

Most employee handbooks might talk generally about discrimination, but very few specifically address age—even when they specifically address other forms of discrimination.

The fix is simple: Add clear, specific language. "We respect workers of all ages"—and list some examples of how you do so. This will send a message to your employees that this is something your organization cares about.

DOES YOUR TEAM ALWAYS PLAN OUTINGS OR PARTIES SUITABLE FOR MILLENNIALS, OR DO THEY PLAN THINGS THAT ARE APPROPRIATE FOR FORTY-SOMETHINGS TOO?

In my years managing younger workers, I've learned many things, some more important than others. One of the things I've learned is that Millennials love to wear costumes, and in my most recent workplace, *every* holiday party we had for a while had a theme. You had to dress up like a lumberjack, wear an ugly sweater, or something like that. The Millennials on my team loved these parties, but a few parties in, the rest of us weren't quite as enthusiastic.

One year, I suggested that the Christmas party should be more traditional—*classier*. We'd dress up, have nice cocktails and champagne, cater the event, and ditch the whole idea of a theme. Everyone kidded me in a warm-hearted way about how old-fashioned it was, but afterward, a huge number of people, *of all ages,* came up to me and privately said, "This is *so* nice. This is elegant. I really like this."

This seems like a trivial point, but the larger concept is one of inclusion: if every party is planned by millennials and designed according to their likes, the non-millennials in the group can't help but feel old and out of place. When I spoke up about how I felt about themed parties, the team responded willingly and inclusively, by changing the party a bit and, in the end, everyone enjoyed themselves and felt comfortable. Parties may not seem like an important thing, but they are; if they make certain people feel older and unwanted and that happens routinely in your organization, you should address it.

IS YOUR OLDER WORKER SUDDENLY LESS ENTHUSIASTIC? PUTTING FORTH LESS EFFORT? FIND OUT WHY, AND MAKE SURE THE PERSON ISN'T FEELING UNDERVALUED OR LEFT OUT.

I've had a lot of older workers tell me that they begin feeling invisible in meetings and group settings. Younger employees don't seem as interested in the older workers' opinions, or they aren't seeking those opinions at all. Consequently, many of these older workers withdraw, and it becomes a self-fulfilling prophecy, where older employees aren't contributing as much as they used to and don't have as much to say.

A smart leader must be tuned into that and take steps to correct it. A well-intentioned leader will model good behavior and find ways to draw the older employee out and find subtle ways to remind the group how valuable this person's perspective is. "Bill, you've experienced a lot of changes in technology at this company. How do you think AI will change how we work?"

When a leader suspects an older worker is feeling invisible, they need to check in with that person and remind them that their opinions and guidance are valuable. You don't know what's wrong if you don't ask.

ARE YOUR FLEXIBILITY PROGRAMS REALLY FOR EVERYONE? OR DO YOU OR YOUR MANAGERS HAVE AN UNCONSCIOUS BIAS?

Many companies boast that they're "family friendly". *If you need to leave early to go to your kid's soccer game, no worries!*

But is your thirty- or forty-something manager as accommodating when an older employee needs to leave early because his aging mother needs him to drop off her medication?

The truth is that older workers often feel like they have less flexibility when they need to take time off for the things they need to do. If your company wants to be family friendly, then it needs to be equally tolerant and welcoming to all its employees. Older workers may no longer have young children who need to be picked up after school, a scenario the boss is likely experiencing himself, but they may have other obligations that are just as vital. They may need to take their eighty-year-old mom to the senior center or to physical therapy. I'm not saying companies should say *no* to these kid-related requests, but I am saying that older workers often feel uncomfortable asking for similar accommodations. That needs to change.

DOES YOUR BUSINESS SEND THE MESSAGE THAT IT'S ALL ABOUT TWENTY-SOMETHINGS?

Look at your website. What images do you choose to represent your company? Are they all shiny young people? Are you guilty of the same misstep the fashion and beauty industry made when it ignored the "real women" of the world?

This is a subtle form of cultural bias: that young is beautiful, and that youth equals optimism and great promise. And it is! It should! But what kind of message does it send to your older workers if they are not physically represented in how you present your company to external audiences?

Companies and organizations have made a conscious effort to show diversity when it comes to gender and race, but we're not seeing anywhere near the same conscious effort to show diversity when it comes to age cohorts.

DO YOU ADDRESS AGE ISSUES AS PART OF YOUR COMPANY'S DIVERSITY AND INCLUSIVENESS EFFORTS?

If you do address ageism in your training, congratulations. You are in a very select group.

I talked to a great number of HR executives for some *very* big companies about this issue. I asked them how often their diversity and inclusion training addresses ageism and combatting ageism, and most admitted that they almost never do. Yet they agreed that ageism should be part of any broad diversity and inclusion strategy.

I also talked with my former associate Pamela Culpepper about this. Pamela has been an HR executive for more than thirty years, including some big-brand beverage companies and financial institutions, and she felt that companies are largely ignoring the issue of ageism in their D&I programs. One reason is that no one is demanding that ageism be included in this kind of training.

"If you don't ask for it, your company won't offer it," she said. "For example, how many companies offer leadership training for their up-and-coming leaders? Most of them do, and that makes sense. Those up-and-coming young people have a longer runway than older workers, so investing in their training makes sense because theoretically these young people will be around for a long time. You can recoup your investment.

On the surface, this makes sense, and is certainly good for the important task of building future leaders, but Pamela cautions that companies need to look at training a little differently, too. For example, what is the cost of not providing training for more seasoned workers? "I can't help but wonder what value we're losing out on by ignoring people from this age group."

Pamela also believes HR can and should play a role in helping a company's leaders become better at leading in ways that value and embrace diverse populations— including older workers. "Will everyone get it? Of course not, but that doesn't mean we shouldn't continue to hold a mirror to our leaders' faces and let them see what's really going on for themselves."

ARE YOU MAKING ASSUMPTIONS AND PRACTICING UNCONSCIOUS BIAS?

Here's what this looks like: When you're making a list of employees who would be good candidates for a certain position, do you unconsciously leave out older employers because you assume the position wouldn't appeal to them? If the job requires a lot of travel, do you discount the older employee because you think the work would be too taxing? If the new position is in Switzerland, do you just assume an older candidate wouldn't be up for the challenge or wouldn't want to leave the home they've been in the last twenty or thirty years?

Executives might not be *physically* scratching names off their list based on these biases, but they might be *unconsciously* leaving names off the list because of their biases.

They make assumptions when they're thinking about who to put on the list, and later, when names of candidates get put on a piece of paper, the older workers are merely left off.

If you want to determine if your organization is ageist, take *age* and substitute it with a specific race or gender. You wouldn't leave African Americans off the list of candidates because you believe blacks don't like to travel, or Hispanics because you think they wouldn't be willing to sell their family home and move to Switzerland, would you? No, of course not—that would be, to put it bluntly, racist.

Then why would you do that to a worker just because he is over fifty?

People who are over fifty are just as unique and different from each other as all people within a certain race are different from each other. You can't make assumptions about them as a group. You must make decisions about them as *individuals*. Above all, those decisions will be infinitely better if informed by actual conversations with employees.

HAVE YOUR HR PRACTICES KEPT UP WITH THE TIMES?

Many companies use what's called a velocity chart to map

out the expected trajectory of a young employee's career. The idea is that you identify your high-potential workers and spend more time grooming them to be great rather than spending time with people who might always be mediocre. You identify these high-potential employees in the first five to seven years of their career and you use the chart to plan career moves for that person. Here's the problem with that—the chart was designed in the 1960s based on the premise that people reach their professional peak in their early fifties.

A lot of companies use this, and it's very well accepted in HR circles. It makes good business sense.

There's a huge problem with it, though: the chart hasn't been updated in *over fifty years*, since it first came out.

When it was first introduced, the assumption was that people would retire at age sixty. But people today are working well past that age. Their life expectancy is much longer. Why haven't we updated this chart? Who honestly believes that the height of a person's career is at age 52?

My friend Sarah pointed this out to me. Older workers are being frozen out of this process, not because of some conscious effort on the part of their HR departments, but because they are not being thoughtful and questioning these old assumptions and practices.

That has to change, too. If you're a CEO or a member of senior management and you're reading this book, you should be pushing your HR department to look into the future and recommend updates to these age-old ways of doing things when needed.

ARE YOU GIVING YOUR OLDER WORKERS A CHANCE TO BE INVOLVED IN SUCCESSION PLANNING?

Most of the HR executives I talked to for this book agreed that most companies don't do succession planning very well. Succession planning is tricky, but if you're an executive and you want to plan for how to replace an older worker, the conversation with that older worker needs to be based on trust and mutual respect.

"The employee has to truly believe the company cares about him or her and values their contributions—past, present, and future—to the organization," Pamela said. "And the respect needs to go both ways. If that is in place, then the conversation about what's next for the employee or about how much longer they see themselves working at the company, and who the older employee thinks would make a good successor—all of those discussions can be positive and productive.

"If the employee feels like you care about her and value her as an employee, you can have this conversation in a productive way. But if that feeling is not there, then the employee is going to feel like you merely want them out of the way. When that happens, you won't have a smooth succession process." The resulting discussion rarely ends well.

ARE YOU ALLOWING SOME STEREOTYPES OF OLDER WORKERS TO FESTER IN YOUR ORGANIZATION?

Here are some common assumptions about older workers and why those assumptions are wrong.

AGEIST STEREOTYPE	FACT
Can't master new skills	Older workers score high in leadership, detail-oriented work, organization, listening, writing, and problem-solving.
Don't understand technology— aren't digital natives	What is a "digital native", anyway? Basically, it's a euphemism for an expensive hire who grew up knowing how to use Snapchat, Twitter, and other social platforms.
Aren't creative	People left in the same job for a long time can become less creative. But put that person in a new job, and she'll come up with new ideas. Mixed-age teams have been shown to be highly productive in areas that require creative thinking like research and development and marketing.
Can't handle stress	Age fosters coping skills. Experience equips older workers to put crisis in context and ride out office drama.
Slow things down	Younger workers can go faster, but they make more mistakes. Older workers may go more slowly—but value accuracy. It's a wash. Output is equal and affected far more by motivation and effort than age.
Miss work because of illness	Older workers are highly reliable. This myth reflects the erroneous cultural association of age with sickness.
Can't handle physically demanding tasks	This is an outdated stereotype. Only a small percentage of jobs require manual labor. Older workers do take longer to recover from workplace accidents but hurt themselves less often.
Are burned out, tired, or unhappy	"Waiting for the gold watch" is a very outdated cliché. People over sixty-five are happiest in their work. Most older workers work because they enjoy their job.

As a people leader for nearly my entire career, for every single one of those stereotypes, I can name a twenty- or thirty-something who demonstrated that same weakness to me in their job performance. How about we just *let go* of all stereotypes, and give honest and direct feedback to all, based on equal criteria?

_____

CHAPTER FOUR

THE DOLLARS & SENSE OF AGEISM IN THE WORKPLACE

I'VE TOLD YOU HOW AGEISM IMPACTED ME, AND how ageism hurts others in your workplace. People feel devalued, marginalized, and dismissed; they feel their identity as a professional, and even as a human, is called into question, and ultimately negated. It's emotionally traumatic, and a harmful example for the younger workers looking to their own future.

Those are the right reasons to care about age bias. But even if you don't care about age bias for the right reasons, you should still care about it for a simple, inarguable reason: *because it's against the law.*

Right now, in our society, those who are marginalized, harassed, or pushed out of their jobs due to ageism largely choose to just let it go, and get on with their lives. Considering the sheer size of the boomer demographic, imagine what would happen if this population of discriminated people decided *not* just to let it go. What would it look like if everyone who was the victim of ageism refused to sit back and take it? What kind of legal liability—and financial exposure—do all companies, regardless of industry, face?

I'm sure you noticed that when the #MeToo movement took hold, it provided a safe place for huge numbers of women to say "no more" not just to incidents going forward, but also to look backward and call out sexism and harassment from their past. Fortunately, many of the companies and organizations named had already made improvements, and could demonstrate progress. I suspect the same will not be true in the case of an #ImNotDone movement.

The potential exposure is *vast*. As a business leader, you can't ignore this risk.

WHAT IS AGE DISCRIMINATION, LEGALLY?

According to the US Equal Employment Opportunity Commission (EEOC), age discrimination involves treating an applicant or employee less favorably because of his or her age. The Age Discrimination in Employment Act, enacted in 1967, forbids age discrimination against people who are age 40 or older. This law prohibits discrimination in any aspect of employment, which includes hiring, firing, pay, job assignments, promotions, layoffs, training, benefits, and any other term or condition of employment.

Despite the clear legal definition, there are many misconceptions about what constitutes age discrimination. People often assume that being a victim of age discrimination means simply that you were suddenly fired outright or laid off because of your age. What I find interesting about the legal definition, though, is that all aspects of a person's employment experience are protected, not just termination. The Act is actually quite broad, and certainly broader than most people realize. For example, if an older worker is treated badly in the workplace, that's age discrimination. And in fact, there's a pattern of that happening more often.

LEGAL CLAIMS OF AGE DISCRIMINATION

Lawsuits, of course, are another sign that your company is ageist. Here are some of the claims that fall under the broad banner of age discrimination:

- Harassment and unwelcome comments by a boss,

peer, or subordinate. If this sort of thing is happening on a consistent basis, that's something that a lawyer will ask about, and will document and include in a claim.

- Favoritism and unfavorable comparison to a younger employee. Do you see your boss continually gravitating towards certain people? Are those certain people consistently younger people?
- Uneven discipline.
- Passed over for promotion past age fifty. If you're someone who has been routinely promoted but those promotions cease when you turn fifty, that may be a sign that your organization is ageist.
- Younger employees being hired after a layoff. Younger people being hired for job postings. Employers have every right to lay people off, but smart companies make sure that when doing large layoffs that they select people from every age cohort so they aren't disproportionately laying off senior workers. When rehiring, though, some companies fail to follow the same policy, and only rehire younger (and cheaper) workers.
- Milestone changes. For example, does something change at work when an employee turns fifty or sixty?
- Discriminatory policies or procedures, such as when family leave is only offered to women of child-bearing age.
- Age-related job notices and advertisements. It's gen-

erally illegal to include age preferences, limitations, or specification in any job notice or advertisement.

· Internships or apprenticeship programs that are too favorable to younger employees.

Each instance alone may not always or irrefutably signal age discrimination, but be aware that this kind of behavior at a company could be used, and *has been used,* against it if someone makes an employment claim.

What is probably the most common form of age discrimination—and more insidious because it is less obvious—is sidelining, marginalizing, or putting an older worker in a role where she no longer has the opportunity to perform at her best. It's believed that a lot of companies take this approach to avoid paying severance. Said another way, they just put people in sub-optimal situations and hope that they'll quit.

When I interviewed lawyers familiar with age discrimination and ageism, they all agreed that being marginalized is legally admissible as evidence of age discrimination. Basically, if it can be proven that sidelining or marginalization is being done differently to someone who's in a protected age group, that's age discrimination.

As I discussed earlier, older workers are typically paid more, so from a pure dollars-and-cents perspective, it makes business sense to get rid of them first. That's a big part of the reason they are being marginalized or pushed out. But if marginalization is practiced systematically, and other solutions aren't even considered, the potential financial blow to the business due to legal liability is *far* higher than potential payroll savings.

Again, I feel strongly about the importance of being good at what you do. I would never argue that someone who isn't performing well deserves to keep his or her job, regardless of age. But most of the people I talked to who felt marginalized or pushed out or were actually pushed out were at senior levels and had never had a bad performance review. If there had been performance issues, they would have been weeded out of the organization already. Thus, there was no indication and no reason for them to believe that it was performance-based.

QUANTIFYING AGE DISCRIMINATION AGAINST A BACKDROP OF UNDERREPORTING

According to the EEOC, the amount of age discrimination complaints has increased dramatically in recent decades. Between 1997 and 2000, approximately 18,000 complaints were filed annually. Since 2008, that number has risen to as high as 25,000 complaints per year, and the number has risen each year. Yes, this increase in complaints likely can be attributed, at least partly, to increased awareness; as people become more aware of what ageism is and what it looks like in the workplace, they're more likely to recognize when they're the subject of discrimination and sue. But more importantly, this rising number reflects the rising age of baby boomers, the largest generation of over-40 workers the country has ever seen. Every year, the number of people *likely to be discriminated against* rises; as a direct result, the legal exposure of every company who employs workers over 40 rises, too.

Even more seriously, employment lawyers across the legal landscape agree: age discrimination is, if anything, vastly under-reported. The reasons for this are probably too numerous, and often too private, to truly know well. Many people who are pushed out of their careers feel ashamed, and don't want to relive that shame through a lawsuit; many more simply feel exhausted and want the ordeal to be over with. Often, the marginalization at work happens over an extended period, and by the time the hammer actually drops, the subject of the ageism has already made new plans and become accustomed to their "new normal"—so reporting the discrimination and filing suit seems like wallowing in a bad situation they'd just as much rather leave behind.

Across the board, though, the most common reason ageism is underreported is that those who have been its victim feel that they don't have enough evidence to make the case for discrimination and won't win a lawsuit. Without the confidence of knowing they have a solid case, it's difficult to subject oneself to the expense, time, and stress of taking their former employer to court. But before anyone breathes a sigh of relief, would you really be able to proudly say you don't have an ageism issue at your company just because you're willing to roll the dice that you won't get sued?

The irony of this lack of reporting is that, based on the data available, it's reasonable to conclude that ageism is in fact *the* most common form of discrimination across US workplaces, more than any other protected class like race or gender. According to a recent report by the Society for Human Resource Management Foundation, two-thirds of older employees say they've seen or experienced workplace discrimination. The AARP concurs; a shocking 64% of workers aged 45 to 75 have been discriminated against based on age. And an overwhelming 92 percent say that age discrimination is "common", according to a 2013 study by the AARP.

Perhaps most persuasive is this figure: in a 2012 AARP survey, 77% of Americans between the ages of 45 and 54 said that they believe *all* employees face age discrimination.

So, why is age discrimination under-reported more than

other forms of discrimination, such as racial and sexual discrimination? If a worker is subjected to racial or sexual discrimination in the workplace, chances are she still has twenty or thirty years' more of work left in her, so it feels worth fighting for. But when it comes to age discrimination, a lot of those with potential claims are close to being ready or willing to retire, so instead, they accept buyouts or packages from the company. There's also another element at work here—pride. If you really feel discriminated against because of your race, gender, or sexual preference, it feels easier to be indignant about that. With age, though, we may start to believe, "well, maybe I'm not as sharp as I once was," or "maybe I'm not as good." Many people hide age discrimination, or just don't talk about it. For them, it's just easier to leave quietly or make it seem like they *chose* to leave than to claim age bias. It's less of an ego blow, to be honest.

Other factors that contribute to underreporting include the fear of retaliation and the sheer amount of time it takes to file a complaint and see it through. As Sue Ellen Eisenberg, one of the attorneys I interviewed, observed:

> The reported numbers are not always accurate. I'm not sure we ever know the full extent of discrimination because it is wholly dependent on reporting. People always want to know the statistics, but do they have any idea how much courage it takes to be part of those numbers? Someone

has to put aside their fear of retaliation and file a charge with the EEOC. And then actually going through the full process of the charge—beyond courage, that takes a lot of time. There are simply no statistics about the number of people who just give up, but it is my belief that it is a very high number.

Many people are trying to prevent a loss of their job and worry that there will be other forms of retaliation against them for filing a complaint, like shunning, being viewed as a rabble-rouser, or just being treated differently if they do keep their job. Again, in Sue Ellen's words, "Not everyone is willing or wants to be a warrior."

It's also a lot of work to file a complaint with the government: a lot of standing in line and waiting. It's not something you can just decide to do and accomplish in a week. It's an emotionally weighty decision that can feel like a decisive bridge-burning one too. Many people, especially those at the tail end of their careers, or who are hoping to keep the door open to continue working with the organization as a consultant, just opt out and choose not to file a complaint at all. Nobody wants an inglorious end to an otherwise glorious career, and what could be more inglorious than suing your employer or an administrator with whom you have a long work history?

As Laurie McCann, a senior attorney with AARP, notes:

Age discrimination is viewed by the courts and society more as an economic issue and we defer to the employer's prerogative. Even employees will say, "Well, it's their business, and I understand why they want to save some money." But you wouldn't say that if the employer said, "We want to save money, so we'll get rid of all of the women," yet we tolerate it when it's age.

According to an AARP study, 61% of participants had seen or experienced age discrimination, yet only 3% made a formal complaint. Remember my comparison to the #MeToo movement? Now we can put a number to it: what if that 58% decided not to sit quietly anymore but instead took action? The #ImNotDone movement could take on momentum like the #MeToo movement; there would be a lot of backward-looking litigation, people losing their jobs for prior instances of age discrimination.

THE REAL COSTS OF AGE DISCRIMINATION

Putting hard numbers around the *costs* of age discrimination is easier. The average cost of a discrimination claim is $125,000, if you choose to settle. If you choose not to settle, the median cost is roughly $200,000. Of those cases that don't settle, 25% result in judgments that exceed $500,000. These figures don't include defense costs, which are typically significant because the average duration of age discrimination matters is 275 days. So, in most cases, you're looking at a defense cost of *at least* the cost of the settlement, and then the settlement or judgment on top of that.

Those are the average cases. Age discrimination can, however, in some circumstances, be much costlier. Consider these two recent examples.

In 2017, a former Lockheed Martin engineer sued for age discrimination after being laid off at age 66 after almost 29 years at the company. He claims that he was a target in a reduction-in-force plan to replace older workers with younger ones, and that he and other older workers consistently received less pay and lower reviews and raises than younger workers. He also said that supervisors and company executives regularly made off-hand remarks about older workers. He was awarded $51.6 million by a jury in a federal court in New Jersey, which may be the highest amount ever awarded to an individual in an age discrimination case.

Also in 2017, Texas Roadhouse, a national, Kentucky-based restaurant chain, was ordered to pay $12 million and furnish other relief to settle an age discrimination lawsuit brought by the EEOC. The EEOC had filed suit seeking relief for a class of applicants the EEOC charged had been denied front-of-the-house positions, such as servers, hosts, server assistants, and bartenders, because of their age, 40 years and older. As part of the settlement, Texas Roadhouse agreed to change its hiring and recruiting practices.

These are extreme examples—very few cases result in judgments that are this high. But they underscore the point that if your company discriminates on the basis of age, you are running a significant and potentially very expensive risk. If a case goes to trial, the plaintiff is a particularly sympathetic person, and the company looks like it has behaved badly or treated an older worker unfairly, the jury can do whatever the hell it wants. And who is to say that the jury hearing the evidence isn't thinking about what will happen to *them* as they get older? If that happens—if they resonate and identify with the plaintiff—you could be facing a judgment or settlement in the hundreds of thousands of dollars, if not millions.

In addition to the actual costs of litigation, you also have to consider the not-insignificant soft costs of age discrimination. These are often hidden and include workplace distractions and loss of productivity for your HR and legal teams, as well as your executives, who have to take time out of their days to deal with these allegations. Even if an employee doesn't file a claim but is merely alleging age discrimination, HR and legal will likely investigate the allegation as a best practice. This means your HR and legal teams' valuable time will be spent interviewing people and reviewing relevant emails rather than on something that would probably be more positive and beneficial for your organization.

Even if a claim is not made public, it's usually no secret to the rest of the organization. It can therefore also significantly impact employee morale.

THE BASIS FOR AGE DISCRIMINATION CLAIMS

When a worker does file an age discrimination claim, they are generally based on one of two primary grounds: harassment or wrongful termination.

HARASSMENT

Harassment can be either implicit or explicit—the common factor is whether you are treating someone who is older differently that you are treating the rest of the workforce. In some cases, this takes the form of a generally dismissive attitude toward older workers, e.g., perceiving them to be less technologically savvy than younger workers. In other cases, it is literally name-calling or using slurs or other offensive language with an older worker (remember those so-called innocuous slurs we previously talked about?)—saying "hey old man," or describing someone as having a "senior moment," can take on legal significance. Taken one at a time, such instances may not sound so bad. But if there is a pattern of such language or treatment happening to an individual, it can negatively influence the individual's self-worth. It also sets up a bad precedent at the company as others begin to assume that such harassment is acceptable. This then perpetuates the pattern.

An important thing to remember about harassment is that determining whether something is offensive turns on the receiver's perception. Even if the employee who uttered the language at issue might have been well-intentioned, if the employee reports it and the employer fails to act in the defense of the victim of such name-calling, claims can be filed and must be legally dealt with, which costs both time and money.

Employers can even be held accountable or liable for harassment by their employees. For example, if an older employee on a manufacturing line complains about something to his boss, and the boss retorts, "Oh, grow thicker skin, it doesn't matter," the employer could be liable if it ever escalated to a lawsuit because the employer allowed employees to behave and treat other people in that discriminatory manner.

The high-end retailer Henri Bendel, when faced with a similar situation, got it right. An older employee had been verbally maligned and disrespected several times by a much younger fellow employee. When she finally complained to her manager, the manager took it right to corporate HR, and the company restated its policy that discriminatory harassment of any kind was not tolerated. As a result, the guy was fired. The company was clear that it just did not tolerate behavior like that, and they nipped it in the bud rather than allowing individual bad behavior to bubble over into something bigger. The woman who had been treated badly will be forever loyal to the company, and as those who know me know, I've always loved the Henri Bendel brand—but now I love them even more!

WRONGFUL TERMINATION

The other type of age discrimination claim turns on wrongful termination. Wrongful termination isn't always a clearly identifiable firing or layoff. More commonly, it's the "make them so miserable they will quit" approach, which I've discussed previously. This can take many forms, such as excluding an older worker from some meetings all of a sudden, giving younger workers plum assignments, better sales territories, or better technology, and making an older worker feel forced to accept a role that isn't a good fit. If there is a pattern of such behavior, it can be interpreted as age discrimination.

Employers take this approach because they don't want to fire the older worker and hope that either the older worker will solve the problem for them by quitting. Some-times they use the "miserable job" as a place to put a worker they deem disposable. More often than not, this is an older employee. One gentleman I spoke with had this happen to him; in the back of his mind, he knew the company wanted him to leave for financial reasons, but he needed the job. As such, when he was asked to take the "miserable job," he said yes. After many months, he asked for a change, and he was told by HR, "Well, you lasted a lot longer than we thought you would!" That was followed by HR telling him there was no other suitable role, so they would "accept his resignation."

This type of ageism is often preceded by psychological damage and general diminishment of the person. Back to my ever-so-wise attorney friend Sue Ellen, who observed:

> All of sudden, once-valued employees feel less valued – they are forced into a role that no longer utilizes their strengths, they aren't invited to key meetings, they are literally and fig-uratively being muted – if not silenced, and it can become a self-defeating cycle because the natural reaction when this happens is to doubt yourself when in reality nothing has changed about your abilities as much as the organization's natural inclination to gravitate towards the next shiny thing. And once that starts to happen to someone it can really wear them down, so this idea of leaving – either voluntarily or not – starts to sound like a plausible idea.

This is essentially what is meant by the infamous phrase "put out to pasture," and it happens much more often to older workers. They are just not involved in the way that they used to be involved, so it becomes this self-defeating cycle of yuck. Because if you're not in the thick of things, your opinions are not going to be as well-informed. Then when you do get the chance to participate or give an opinion, it might not be as savvy or as spot-on as it used to be because you have started to doubt yourself and your ability to deliver value.

As humans, we are at our happiest when we feel involved, valued, and needed. When you no longer feel that in your workplace, particularly as an older worker who has been invested in a career for 30 or 40 years, it feels almost like a loss of *identity*. It's almost like the stories you hear of one spouse dying followed quickly by the other. And after interviewing dozens of people, I can confirm that it hurts. A lot. Their hurt was palpable in each and every one of my interviews.

It's a real ego blow to be treated this way. It's hurtful. These are people who have spent most of their careers being highly valued, and then they all of a sudden get to a place where they start to wonder, *when did I become invisible?*

I think that's partly why I opted to move on when I experienced this myself. I got some really good advice from a senior-level recruiter who I've known for a long time: he said, "The minute it [staying in the job] starts to erode your self-confidence, you have to get out of there."

I'm blessed with a fair degree of self-confidence, and it's a lot easier for me than I think it is for a lot of people. I was also in a position where I *could* quit—that's not true for everyone.

Age discrimination also takes a heavier toll than other forms of discrimination on the health of victims. Boomers who want to keep working often need the income and health insurance that comes with full-time employment. Taking that away from them places a greater burden on public resources. In a statistic that shocked and horrified me, according to the AARP, those who lose their jobs past age 58 are at the greatest health risk, and on average, lose three years of life expectancy if they don't find another job.

A work study conducted by AARP in 2017 found that age is the leading reason for negative treatment by an employer. Participants were asked: "Thinking about how you are personally treated in the workplace, would you say the following generally caused your employer to treat you better, worse or no differently: age, race/ethnicity, gender, disability, sexual orientation, religion, veteran status?" Notably, age was the leading reason, and it was nearly double race and *more than double* gender. This underscores the negative psychological and physical effects experienced by older workers subject to age discrimination.

AGE DISCRIMINATION IN HIRING

According to the U.S. Bureau of Labor Statistics, nearly half of those who've been out of a job for six months or more are over 50. It is an undeniable truth that it's much harder to find a job when you're over 50, but it's also hard to prove. When you're on a job search, it feels like you're putting hundreds of resumés out there, and they're going into a black hole. When you don't get a response from a company, you have no insight into who *did* get called for an interview, or why; as such, it's hard to prove that age was any kind of factor.

Similarly, sometimes the employers themselves don't even see older candidates because they're being screened out by recruiters and employment agencies. This can be dangerous—ultimately, it's the *company* that bears the legal risk for age discrimination in hiring.

One recruiter with whom I spoke, Elizabeth Zea of JUEL, says that professional longevity can sometimes be held against a candidate, but there are creative ways on a resume to ensure experience doesn't get in the way of getting a first meeting. "I do see resumes on which college graduation dates are not included, nor the early employment years of a career. This can be effective if a candidate wants the focus to be on their most recent professional experience rather than their tenure in the market."

Elizabeth doesn't think employers are necessarily overtly ageist. "No client has ever told me, 'I only want to interview young people,' but they will say they want a 'rising star' or 'someone whose career is ascending.'"

I asked Elizabeth if it's a money or budget issue, and she acknowledges it often is. "There are definitely age-50+ candidates willing to take less money, and they are at a point in their careers where they can do that; but we need to help them come up with confident and powerful ways to express that, because too often, 'I can make less' translates into 'I'm desperate' and no one wants to hire desperate."

Perhaps part of the #ImNotDone mission needs to include coming up with new language and new ways to talk about more options for experienced job candidates.

A hiring manager for a large sales company clued me in on some other potentially ageist behavior that he has seen when he brings older candidates in for interviews. "The feedback I often get is something like, 'so and so is great, has tons of relevant experience, but I just don't think they are a cultural fit.'" What does that mean, exactly? Does that mean that if in your company most people don't have families to go home to, the prospective employee who has to catch the 5:04 to get home before the daycare closes will not be a good cultural fit?

As an employer, preventing age discrimination at the hiring stage is key. Make sure that you are doing diversity and inclusion training that includes respecting a multigenerational workforce, working proactively to prevent discrimination and harassment, and working on things like unconscious bias.

As the saying goes, an ounce of prevention is worth a pound of cure. If you are ever faced with an age discrimination lawsuit as an employer, your lawyer will be able to point to these steps as evidence that you view diversity and inclusion in the broadest way possible and are taking steps to address it proactively.

THE ELEPHANT IN THE ROOM

As we've established, it's a fact that older workers tend to cost companies more. Especially older workers who have had a successful career because, as they've advanced, they've been financially rewarded. At a certain point, the cost-benefit analysis may no longer work out in favor of the worker. But that's not a reason to lose that worker. It's an opportunity to open the door to a discussion—a discussion that just might lead to a win/win situation.

The vast majority of older, highly-compensated workers with whom I've spoken are open to a conversation about continuing to work for potentially less money, as long as they get to be a part of that conversation. This likely will surprise you so I am going to repeat it—your senior, highly-compensated employees are open to talking about compensation. So yes, compensation level might be the elephant in the room, but you can solve it if you choose to. As an employer, you have to try to keep these high-value senior people around as long as possible. It's the right thing to do, it's respectful, it's a way of being gracious to them for a long career.

Yes, you are running a business, and every employee regardless of her age has to prove her value. But just because an employee is expensive doesn't mean you shouldn't ask, *am I using her in the right way? Would she be open to a different form of compensation? Should we have a five-year off-ramp for her so that she can get her financial house in order?*

Many companies offer a buyout of sorts, an early retirement, which is usually offered to workers who have a combination of age and years of experience. On the face of it, this seems like a win-win for everyone. And in the short term, maybe it is. The employer sees some short-term savings by losing the people with the most generous compensation, and the employee gets some financial incentive to leave her job. But how the buyout is structured and positioned to employees says a lot. It may be a "voluntary" buyout, but if the alternative to not taking it is a demotion, or a message that you are now taking your chances with an upcoming reduction in force (read: *we're kicking you out, one way or another*), if the employer is only offering this to workers in their 50s and 60s, it's going to feel like age discrimination, and it very well might be.

Over the course of my career, I have seen this happen more than a dozen times. Sometimes it works, and sometimes it backfires. One such company had promised Wall Street a huge cost reduction over a period of many years. After rounds of layoffs, the company still had a long way to go to achieve the salary synergy they had promised, so they opted to offer voluntary packages. People felt like it was a bird in the hand they should take to avoid the possibility of a layoff in the not-too-distant future. While they offered packages broadly, the only people who could realistically afford to take it were those aged 50+. Many called it age discrimination—but did so on their way out the door. In the end, the company lost considerable institutional knowledge, but even more good will, because people felt that they were just pushing out everybody that had a long history with the company.

Smart companies who are fearful of litigation may simply offer a package to everybody. The problem with this approach is you have a bunch of Millennials who will happily take the money, go travel the world, and then come back and get another job!

So, when I talk about the long run, I'm suggesting that a business leader consider not just the dollars and cents saved by losing your older employees today, but also the other implications of mass restructurings, especially if they disproportionately affect a certain group of people.

We also have to consider that the standard narrative that older workers cost more may not even be as true as it once was. When I was coming up in the business world, you just expected that you would get a five- to seven-percent raise every year to account for increases in the cost of living. When you can start making six figures, your salary begins to jump exponentially under that model, and you can become very expensive. Now, though, progressive companies are moving away from a tenure-based compensation model toward a largely incentive-based one. This means that the salaries they pay their workers are based primarily on both the employees' performance and the company's performance. In fact, 90 percent of large companies now use incentive-based compensation, which is a staggering 78 percent increase from 2005. Rather than buy into the idea that older workers necessarily cost more money, perhaps business owners should instead consider changing up their incentive structure a bit.

Another relevant consideration is that nobody really has pensions anymore. Pensions used to be a huge carrying cost for companies, especially because employees are living so much longer. But only 22 percent of companies—which represents a 68 percent decrease—actually offer anything at all that looks like a pension, and most of it is employee-funded. So that's another traditional narrative we can call bullshit on—pensions do not make older workers more expensive.

What about the increased health care costs to companies as a result of carrying older workers on their books? It's true that healthcare generally costs more for older workers, but the difference is not huge. Also, and perhaps surprisingly, recent data indicates that health care costs for people between ages 50 and 64 increased at a rate of only 4 to 6 percent, as compared to an increase of 7 to 8 percent for those employees in the 25 to 49 age bracket. My guess is that a lot of that has to do with the fact that older workers have grown kids who are out the house, so they are no longer, for example, paying for their braces. To say that your healthcare costs are necessarily going to go up if you have older workers is an additional fallacy that needs to be considered when assessing the real costs of employing older workers.

EMPLOYEE ENGAGEMENT

There is yet another business case to be made for keeping older workers around, and that's employee engagement. We hear this term a lot explained in many different ways, but really, it just means "do your employees give a damn?" When they do, everything is better in the workplace, whether it's a product or a service that you are offering. It's the notion that satisfied and engaged employees are going to make your company look good.

Research by Gallup found that workers in their 50s actually have higher engagement scores than workers in their 30s. Honestly, this doesn't surprise me because older workers are usually there because they want to be there. Money, although still a motivating a factor, is just not as important to them as it once was.

What does this mean for companies? Consider this example: a mid-size company with average employee engagement scores, $5 billion in sales, $800 million in operating margin, and $400 million total shareholder return could stand to achieve a $300 million increase in sales, a $32 million increase in operating margin, and a $24 million improvement in total shareholder return, if that company improved its employee engagement levels to best-in-class levels.

So: as you're weighing the dollars and sense of keeping older employees in your workforce, it bears considering that older workers will bring more engagement to the table, and more engagement means your company stands to make more money. It's a win-win.

CHAPTER FIVE

IN THEIR OWN WORDS

I INTERVIEWED DOZENS OF PEOPLE WHO HAD EXPE-rienced or witnessed age discrimination, and I received feedback to my blog from another hundred. I'm going to tell a few of their stories here, because I think it's import-ant to deeply understand the human side of ageism.

Some people I interviewed were willing to allow me to use their name, and others, for reasons I fully respect, were not. For the sake of consistency, I opted not to use any names. I was inspired by journalist and author Bob Woodward's words about his sources for his recent book. He believes that using unnamed sources is necessary "to get to the real truth."

Just like his, my sources are not anonymous to me. I know exactly who they are, and I am ever so grateful that they trusted me to tell their story.

When a group of people experiences the same traumatic event, a car crash, for example, they may each perceive it somewhat differently. Some people remember the sights and sounds. Others recall the emotions, the pain, or the fear. Some try to block it. Almost all think about what the long-term repercussions will be.

The same is true of the way victims of ageism perceive and recall their experiences. Each person tells a story based on different facts, but almost all of them share certain similarities. The feelings of being marginalized, discounted, underutilized, and abandoned are poignant and consistent. Those emotions are especially intense after a long and productive career in which a person has contributed so much value to an organization, only to be cast aside when they reach a certain age.

Every story of ageism is different, yet there are remarkable similarities. I thought it would be worthwhile to hear from some of the victims. These are all proud, talented, accomplished people. In fact, they probably dislike being referred to as victims. But in a very real sense, they are. They're victims of the one remaining form of workplace discrimination that is still socially acceptable.

As you read their stories, I am sure you will recognize similarities to your own story, or to the story of a family member, or maybe someone who works at your company. These people don't want your pity; they wouldn't accept it. But they also know their stories are illustrative of the serious social and professional problem of ageism, and there is value in sharing those stories.

WILLIAM

William is a great example of how even the most talented employees can become the target of ageism. He was an award-winning creative at a large advertising agency. Over his thirty-plus-year career his work received many professional accolades, he was extremely well compensated for his talent, his clients respected him, his junior associates were inspired by him, and his employer highly valued his contributions to the company.

When William was forced out at age fifty-five, at the top of his game, he wasn't even surprised. In a way, he sort of rationalized it. He told me he understood; he said, "My salary was too high, and we had just had a big cut in a client budget. They can't afford me."

I challenged him on that. I said, "But, William, if you were forty-five years old instead of fifty-five, don't you think the company would find something else for you to do?"

They never questioned William's talent, they just made the decision that he was nearing the end of his career—with no input from him.

In response to my "is ageism a thing" question, William says that ageism is absolutely real, and he's living proof it doesn't just affect women. It's not a gender or ethnicity issue. William says, "If you are part of another protected class, for example, based on disability, religion, country of origin, or skin color, more thought is given before a company will terminate your employment. But if you're a white male over fifty years old, they don't think twice about it. They don't have to. If you're an ethnic minority, they'll at least think twice, but probably do it anyway."

William also brought up a larger societal issue that he believes contributes to ageism. We live in a throw-away society. If we no longer have any use for a piece of furniture, or an old cell phone, or a household item, we toss it in the trash. If we don't need it, we dump it. William theorizes that our throw-away society normalizes a mindset that employees are disposable. For example, if an older employee lacks social media analytics skills, rather than train that employee, they choose to just discard them and hire someone new (read: younger).

It's a common experience for older employees to self-identify as potential targets for ageism, and then worry about what's coming. William says, "I knew my agency was challenged financially with some lost businesses, lost accounts, and knew I was paid at a senior level, which I should have been because it was tied to my experience and the value I brought. But I also knew that that made me highly vulnerable. Since when should succeeding and achieving throughout one's career become a liability? But I knew it was."

When the ageism began, it was subtle. In the agency business, meetings with clients are a very important part of the job. One day, William noticed that he wasn't invited to an important meeting... with *his* client. He knew his work wasn't subpar, because his colleagues were showing the client *his* work. "Nobody told me anything. They just stopped inviting me into the room."

William says the subtlety was insidious. "Here's the problem with all of the -isms, whether it's racism, sexism, ableism, or ageism; it's just so f-ing subtle, and a lot of people don't even see it when it's happening to them. Furthermore, the perpetrators sometimes don't even realize they're doing it. But it doesn't make it any less real. I could count on one hand the number of employees in the creative department over the age of fifty. If you're in your forties, you should be saving your money."

DIANA

Diana built a long and successful career in the marketing services business, which she says is very much a young person's game. Diana would look around the office at the other employees and realized she was decades older than they were and she absolutely loved it. "I'd look around and realize I could have given birth to almost every one of them. I loved them, and they loved me. But there is a dark side to it, and in our business where youth dominates, you can't hide from it. That's why I made it a personal goal to always be relevant." But with that commitment to stay relevant came some very natural anxiety about her potential for continued future employment as a woman over 50.

It turned out that her anxiety was well founded. "I didn't feel old in my forties. Age didn't bother me. In fact, I probably felt the strongest and best I ever did as I was turning fifty. But I'll never forget; I was having dinner with our CEO, and he asked me out of nowhere how old I was. I thought, *Where the hell did that come from?* I doubt very much he was asking men the same question." Do women potentially face both ageism and sexism above the age of fifty? You bet.

Diana believes there is still a pervasive, male-centric belief in the workplace that women executives don't really need to work because their husbands are probably also successful. The wife's salary is just "extra." While that may be true in a small percentage of cases, most women rely on their salaries to feed a family, put kids through college, and save for retirement. And lots of professional women are, in fact, the lead breadwinner in their household; far out-earning their husbands. And let's not forget that growing category of professional women who opted not to marry. So, the loss of a job in a woman's fifties—her peak earning years—can be devastating.

When Diana was forced out of the company she helped build and grow, it was handled poorly, and I asked her what they could have done differently? "How about everything! If they really needed or wanted me to go, they could have treated me with dignity and respect and they could've allowed me to graciously figure out a way to exit. And a little transparency would have helped too, instead of making me miserable, so I would want to quit."

Even if Diana's salary and role had to be reduced, there are ways to approach the situation that apparently don't occur to employers. "I imagine how it could have been. The CEO could have said, 'How can we take advantage of what you have to offer. You've built something for us, but now we need to transition what you built to the next generation. How can we make this work for you and for us?' Wouldn't that have been nice?"

A respectful transition may also have saved Diana's

employer a lot of money. When employees are forced out for illegal reasons, legal consequences often ensue. "I felt like I had to consult a lawyer. Now we both have lawyers getting involved and turning it into an unpleasant back and forth costing time and money. I kept asking myself, *how did I get here?*"

Even more worrisome than losing her income was losing her health insurance. These days, buying health insurance on the open market for a family can cost as much as a mortgage payment. Diana says, "In the past, people retired with full pensions and full health insurance in their late fifties. Things are different now. Most of us can work well into our sixties and seventies—and want to... and *need* to. When you push someone out in their mid-fifties they don't qualify for Medicare for another decade. Even if we are completely healthy, we still need medical care. The only thing harder than losing a job in your mid to late fifties is getting another one. Not having healthcare is a huge worry. Huge."

Diana also said the younger employees in her firm knew exactly what was happening to her. One young superstar in his twenties said to her, "I guess I better get out of here before I get too old." Companies would be wise to think twice about how they exit their older employees, because the young employees are watching and taking note.

MARY LOU

It's important to point out in this book that ageism is not something only people in their fifties and beyond need to be concerned about. Although I do hope ageism is a distant memory by the time Millennials are middle-aged, we can't count on it. No matter what your age, you will eventually join the ranks of the fifty-somethings, and you probably should have a strategy. Mary Lou is a good example.

Mary Lou is a forty-something executive for a communications agency. She told me she worries about ageism. She said, "I often find myself wondering how do I make this agency life work when I have gray hair? The average age where I work is probably 28. I'm in my forties and I need and want to work for at least another decade or two. Will I be able to? What will happen to me then? I know I am not in the crosshairs yet, but I look around and can't help but feel I will be."

We've all seen it happen right in front of our eyes. Maybe we only had a vague notion of what was going on, but we knew something was up. Mary Lou told me, "I've seen a lot of people, both men and women, get moved to the sidelines or leave altogether throughout my career. For a long time, I think I was somewhat oblivious to what was going on. I just assumed the ones on the sidelines weren't any good, and that the ones leaving were happily going.

Now that I am in a senior role, I know better. I can clearly see that's not it at all, and I'm bothered by that. We should all be bothered by that."

She also doesn't understand the business logic. "We are living through a time of tremendous change in the agency business, and so are our clients. We are living in a constant state of transformation, and it isn't going away. The people who have lived through major transformation, seen and weathered seismic shifts—they've figured out how to put the right talent in place to manage this change, yet the very people I need right now are the ones made to feel not relevant. What can be more relevant than managing transformation?"

What is interesting to me about Mary Lou's story is this: Mary Lou is still working in her job, and she has not been forced out. No one can say, "Oh she's just angry, or bitter, or not good at her job." She's well respected, talented, and very successful. But she's still worried about ageism. She has deep empathy for all victims of ageism, and the effects it can have on an organization.

Mary Lou cautions, "As employers, we need to remember that everyone is looking for cues from the organization's leadership about what they value and how they treat people. When the answer is 'not well,' part of the natural response is 'Phew, I'm glad it isn't me,' but lurking inside is also the thought, 'But someday it could be me.' When employees watch the organization treat long-time workers unfairly, they become wary and mistrusting." That is certainly not in the best interest of either the employee or the employer.

BRIAN

Brian is a good example of what happens when you're approaching fifty and you're out in the job market looking for employment. In a word, it's tough. Some might say it's brutal. In addition to all of the normal hurdles to getting a job that all job seekers of every age have to go through, there's also the worry that your age is working against you. Does ageism affect people in their forties and fifties who are job hunting? It absolutely can, but the worst part is that you will probably never know.

Brian is a forty-something professional who found himself in job search mode when a company he was working for shut down. He did everything right in his job search. He polished his resume. He networked. He applied to openings online. He was a highly qualified candidate and he knew it. But after a while, he felt something was wrong. His resume was working, but he wasn't getting past the first interview.

He told me, "Unfortunately, I've been in a situation

where my job has been eliminated more than once in the last five or six years, which means I've had to look for jobs a lot. Sadly, my eyes have been opened to all the subtle ways that prospective employers dance around the age issue. Did anyone come out and tell me I was too old? No. But after a while when you keep getting asked about your 'digital skills,' even though the job has nothing to do with that, it starts to send a message."

Many employment agencies will counsel older job seekers to remove from their resume the year they graduated from college. But in the age of the Internet, finding out someone's age usually takes just a quick Google search. If an employer is covertly attempting to determine a job applicant's age, that does not necessarily mean ageism is at play. It may be connected to salary. Potential employers might try to determine a job applicant's age in order to predict what level of salary they might expect. Younger candidates have a distinct advantage here; employers know they'll work for lower salaries.

EMMA

Emma is in her forties and works for a global Fortune 100 company. She is gainfully employed, getting great reviews and accolades, but she's worried. The company she works for recently moved and redesigned its headquarters—not just the offices, but also the staff. Management said the move was designed to attract "younger talent."

"It was so clear and so obvious that anything 'old,' including the people, was no longer welcome in the 'new' company. I mean, I get it, the company had to change and evolve, but it couldn't have been more obvious. We literally told our people that we were designing our entire corporate headquarters in a way to attract younger talent. I'm all for younger talent, but there has to be a blend."

Emma noticed that the vast majority of the new hires were in their twenties. And all the people leaving were in their fifties. Not being terribly far from the big 5-0 herself, she couldn't help but feel a bit concerned. She said, "Well, it's pretty hard not to feel like you might not be welcome after a certain age when every conversation we have is about attracting young talent and finding young digital talent."

Here's where Emma's story gets interesting. She was having drinks with a group of peers and friends, something they often did for fun; but this time, it was different. She told me, "We all looked at each other and realized with some relief that we'd all survived the transition of multiple layoffs. But the relief quickly dissipated, because being among the few "old people" left made us feel vulnerable. We committed then and there to stick together, and what started out as drinks became a support group with a purpose. We saw that when you're fifty, you're quite likely going to get screwed. So, now when we get together, we try to figure out what will be the best role to be in when that happens."

Emma said the company leadership was hoping, through all of their organizational changes, that they would have a natural attrition of many of the older employees who didn't want to change and adapt. "I absolutely agree that it is hard for a company to move forward with employees who won't or can't change, I just wish we had spent as much time trying to help people cope with change as we did trying to get them to leave." In Emma's ideal world, best-in-class companies manage change in a way that is inclusive and respectful to all.

If you ever met Emma, you would agree with me that she's the epitome of the type of person any organization should want to hire. But here she is, wondering how much time she has left. While she might feel her job is secure at the moment, she's smart enough to start thinking beyond the next several years.

NANCY

As I discussed earlier, eliminating ageism is good for business. But the emotional benefits for people are also deeply important to consider. In my opinion, and proven true by experience, caring about other people, and especially your employees, is a competitive advantage for any business. When employees feel the sting of ageism it is deeply painful. For so many older workers, ageism ends their careers in a way that is unpleasant, to say the least. They end up being forced out through no fault of their own, simply because they're too expensive, or *perceived* to be too old.

Nancy worked full-time for a top agency, until financial considerations caused management to decide that there were too many senior, expensive employees on the payroll, and cuts had to be made. Nancy was fifty-five at the time, and she was one of my direct reports. I was able to make a case to keep her, but only if her salary was reduced through bringing her work to part-time status. When she agreed, I breathed a huge sigh of relief, as I felt I had saved her job and kept valuable expertise at the agency.

After I left my job and decided to write about this topic, I approached Nancy about being interviewed. Initially— understandably, I think—she was reluctant, but I assured her that nothing was off-limits, and I wanted her candor. In our very first conversation, we talked about how I, as her manager, had handled her situation. She told me, "It was the right move for me, but at the time, I felt like I didn't have any choice in the matter, and so honestly, it didn't feel very good."

Ouch. I thought I had handled it well. But I did *not* do exactly what I have now learned is so important—have an open and honest discussion with the employee. I also did something I think far too many managers are guilty of; since she "agreed" to the part-time choice, I never had to tell her that her full-time job would have been eliminated. *Phew,* I thought to myself, *I avoided a difficult conversation.*

What I now know is that I also deprived Nancy of the opportunity to know all the background. I failed to treat her like the seasoned and mature professional she was, and still is.

We moved on from that circumstance in our conversation, and I'm glad we did, because Nancy spoke very directly and powerfully about the pain of what had happened to her after I left.

Nancy told me, "I think the worst part of ageism is that you just feel invisible. Literally invisible. And it gets worse as you get older." She told me of the pain and embarrassment she had felt during a recent time when her boss walked right by her desk to seek input from people more junior than her and talked about personnel—a discussion she used to be a part of. "I'll be honest, when that happens and you aren't even acknowledged, it hurts. It's hard. I have other examples like that. On some level, they may feel like petty and small examples, but they add up and send a signal that is hard and often humiliating."

Nancy makes a good point. Often ageism doesn't reveal itself in one meeting, or one incident at the office. It's cumulative. She told me, "It's been very damaging, and, in many ways, it is the accumulation of lots of little things. It feels a bit like death by a thousand cuts. It is the first time in my career that I have felt marginalized and therefore disrespected and irrelevant."

Nancy said others in her office noticed how the boss was so dismissive of her. "The impact on the rest of the organization shouldn't be ignored. When the boss walks by me and talks to the junior people they are uncomfortable, too. They see how I am being treated and know it isn't right. It is noticeable and hurtful to the culture of the organization."

There will always be individual people who make the wrong choices in any organization. Ultimately, though, Nancy blames top management for allowing ageism in any form in the workplace. "The buck stops with the people running the show—the executive team—and if they aren't paying attention, and don't notice those behaviors, then shame on them."

ALICE

Alice went to work for a very well-known social media company when she was 49. Her star seemed to ascend rapidly—she was advising senior people in the company and was given more and more plum assignments. When Alice turned 50, her daughter sent her a balloon bouquet. "Happy 50th!" screamed the balloons.

"It was at that point that I realized that nobody in the company had any idea how old I was. I used to get continual positive affirmation, and hear things like, 'How did you know that? That's amazing,' and, 'That's so smart.' It was crazy, but after my 50th birthday celebration, the conversation literally changed overnight. I am blessed with good genes, and I look much younger than my age. The prevailing conversation switched from my work to one about how I looked. Now my coworkers were asking, 'How do you stay so young?' and, 'Your skin looks great, have you had surgery?'"

This switch baffled and slightly amused Alice, but what she found most alarming was much more real. She noticed that the nature of the assignments she was getting seemed to change a little bit. "They were just a little less meaty. But when I knew for sure was when a big new product launch was coming, for a product I'd helped develop, I was given someone to co-lead with. I had never before been asked to co-lead with anybody."

Her co-leader was 29 years old. As she put it, youth is very valued in this particular company, so it wasn't at all surprising to work with somebody so young, and in fact, she had many young colleagues who she thinks are brilliant and are going to rule the world someday, but what was definitely not typical for her was to co-lead the project as opposed to being the single leader of the project.

Over the next year, the same thing happened to her more and more, and she said that she felt marginalized, a word that I've heard a lot of other people I interviewed use. "I have always taken a lot of pride in my work. I know I'm good. But I was becoming less and less satisfied and feeling less and less valuable, so I quit."

When Alice quit, she was 52 and looking for a job in Silicon Valley. She told me she had a very difficult time finding a comparable job, but eventually she found one. "I'm relatively happy. I'm making less money, but I don't feel like I have to walk around the organization being paranoid about my age."

THE NEED TO BE VALUED

The desire to be valued and validated in the workplace seems to be a universal human need. It may be surprising, but for the people I spoke to, that basic need was just as important, if not more important, than the actual size of their paycheck. Older workers tend to value stability. They don't want to be put out to pasture at age fifty-six, fifty-seven, or fifty-eight. Finding a new job at that age is much more difficult. It's a vulnerable time.

Unfortunately, many of the people I interviewed for this book complained of a conspiracy of silence. There is an unwillingness to talk about career options for otherwise talented workers once they hit a certain age. Men and women I interviewed would tell me they received excellent performance reviews and work evaluations for years, and they knew their work exceeded expectations. But gradually they just began to feel that something was off. Eventually, they noticed they were being included less and replaced in meetings by younger colleagues. The opportunities that had been available to them years before had dried up and disappeared, even though they were doing the best work of their lives. As one victim of ageism told me, "The rules seemed to shift. But no one told me."

A CEO can put a stop to it in their own company, but on a macro level, there are no simple solutions to ageism in our society. I just want everyone in a leadership role in every organization to understand the benefits of keeping older employees in their jobs. Yes, there are some things that younger workers can do that perhaps older workers generally can't—but the reverse is also true!

Older workers bring valuable insight and the wisdom of experience—which most younger employees simply cannot match. In my opinion, a blended workforce with employees of all ages is the best of both worlds. In the right environment, set by the CEO, when older and younger workers can coexist and learn from each other, the entire organization benefits.

CHAPTER SIX

WISDOM, EXPERIENCE, AND CONNECTIONS

KEEPING OLDER WORKERS ON YOUR TEAM IS NOT a zero-sum game, or at least it doesn't have to be. You're not hurting your company or younger workers by maintaining an older workforce.

In fact, having a combination of young, energetic people working with older, seasoned people can produce magical results. No matter what business you are in when you combine the wisdom and experience of age with the exuberance and open-mindedness of youth, the result is often innovative ideas delivered in a savvy, strategic way.

One example was the time our team was making a pitch to a longtime client, a company that has been a beloved institution for almost a hundred years. The ideas from our young, on-fire creative department were fantastic—perhaps a little out there, but fresh and wildly creative. I couldn't wait for the pitch. But when we met with the client, I could tell some of the company's executives were a little uncomfortable with the approach we were suggesting for them. I sensed this—not because I'm brilliant or knew the executives in the room, but because I'd been in a lot of rooms like this and had done a lot of pitches. I could see our ship was losing the wind and drifting off course a bit.

My experience not only enabled me to read the room, but it also gave me the chutzpah to step in, interrupt the flow of the pitch, and redirect it. I merely gave it a little nudge to make these beautiful ideas a little more palatable to the execs for this particular client. Very soon, our ship started to ride a little higher in the water. Our sails filled with a fresh wind. I could see the clients beginning to smile more and arch their eyebrows with interest in the pitch we were making. They were getting it. They liked it.

I never in a million years would have expected my young creative guy to know how to do that—course correct in that way—but I knew to do it because of all the years I'd spent in situations just like this.

Diana calls that combination of creative youth and savvy wisdom the "special sauce" that every company wants. "When you marry youth and wisdom," she says, "it's is a powerful combination."

When I look back on my career, I can honestly say that I've seen that particular combination work time and again and it is among my favorite work experiences. I vividly remember one of my career experiences when I was on the "youth" side of that. When I was twenty-two, and right out of college, one of my first assignments was to serve on a strategic planning team for Dow Chemical. It was just me and a bunch of much older men. I went into the first meeting thinking, "I don't know what I'm doing. I don't know what I'm talking about. What can I tell these guys that they don't already know?" But these guys welcomed my input. They valued what I said because my ideas were different from their own and as a result, we did some great work together. To this day, thirty some odd years later, I still have my notebook from that project and vividly remember how much I enjoyed working with those men and how much they taught me.

Sometimes wisdom can be a great match, not just with youth, but also with inexperience. When I rejoined Dow decades later to lead communications it was because the company wanted a bold new approach to building its brand. The CEO himself told me I was starting with a clean slate and that I had a clear mandate for change. I knew exactly *what* to do, but after a few months realized that I needed the wisdom of my colleagues to know *how* to do it. I think I would expand on Diana's view; wisdom is a special sauce when added to any situation.

Susan Credle had a similar experience. Susan is a wildly talented and extremely successful Global Chief Creative Officer for FCB, a global advertising agency. Susan is often the one whose wisdom is sought. But when she was brought in to her current agency, her predecessor had retired. Based on stereotypes, and the reality that she was brought in to make some changes, Susan might have expected this man to be tired or creatively dried up, but to the contrary, she welcomed his advice, counsel *and* his creative chops. He quickly became a valuable mentor. He shared his experience and expertise with Susan, but more importantly, he was honest.

"One thing I very much value about more senior people is that they're not trying to prove themselves or anything else anymore," Susan said. "You just get complete honesty. What a rare gift that is."

He continues to advise Susan when she asks for it.

"His wisdom and insight are truly incredible," she said. "It would have been naïve and misguided of me not to want him around. We clicked right away, and I eventually told him that he was welcome to be part of our global creative councils in perpetuity."

As someone who came up in the industry when there was very little diversity, Susan has long been a vocal champion for women in advertising. But she certainly does not turn a blind eye to the issue of ageism.

"Look, I get it; we are in a youth-dominated business and so are many of our clients, so I know that we haven't always done a good job of showing older people that we do value them and their input." And she knows it is good for business. "The odds are, if you bring me a problem, I've seen it solved incorrectly and I've seen it solved correctly so I can help others solve their issues faster and better. As business leaders, we need to know enough to actually see and value that wisdom. It may not look like the output we are used to seeing, but it has tremendous value to the next generation who will be more agile, more interesting and more productive, because a seasoned professional has mentored them through it."

Susan also embraces her responsibility as a leader to come up with unique solutions. "There is no such thing as a specific age when your creativity dries up, but there may be an age where looking at the job a little differently might be a good idea. We have a writer in his 60s, and we've created a great role for him. While the industry might say his time has come and gone, his work was recently recognized with a Cannes Lion at the industry's most important global awards show. When talent is used the right way, there is no expiration date."

None of these stories of young people collaborating with older coworkers surprises me. When I look back on my years in the agency business, some of my closest collaborations were with people twenty or thirty years younger than me. These relationships were based on mutual respect; I respected they were not coming from where I came from, and they appreciated the same in me. We listened to each other. I was a mentor to them, but they were mentors for me as well. The learning never stops.

PRESSURE TO RETIRE

Unfortunately, some older workers worry about reaching a time in their careers when they are not valued or considered as relevant as they once were. Their coworkers aren't bashful about asking them when they plan to retire or why they are waiting so long to retire, and these older workers begin to develop a fear of being put out to pasture. They make the decision to retire before someone else makes the decision for them.

As the owner of her own successful law practice, there

was no one who could pressure Sue Ellen to retire, but she understands what it feels like all the same. People started asking her when she was going to retire when she was only in her mid-fifties. She hadn't thought much about retirement until that point, and she knew the questions were well-intentioned, but she couldn't help but think more about it when so many were asking about her plans. She wasn't sure when she would retire, but she knew she would continue to work as long as her skills continued to improve and her contributions were meaningful.

But then, as her mid-fifties became her mid-sixties, she realized that her skills weren't eroding at all. In fact, she realized she was becoming a *better* attorney as she got older, not worse. The years of experience and the confidence that came from an expanded track record of success were making her more effective.

"I'm a much better lawyer than I was even ten years ago," she said. "I've had that much more experience dealing with clients, judges, juries and everyone else. If I'm a client, why wouldn't I choose a sixty-something attorney with all this experience and knowledge?"

Sue Ellen built her career by selling herself as the best attorney for her client, and she continues to do that. She believes the US must shift its cultural attitudes about age.

"We need to learn from other cultures," she said. "In many African countries, old age is revered. You wouldn't dream of making a major decision without consulting an elder. That would be ignoring valuable history and knowledge. Why would you pass up that opportunity? It belies rational understanding. Yet that is what businesses do every day as they systematically force older people out of the organization."

LEAVING AGEISM AT THE DOOR

After I left my job, many of my younger former coworkers kept in touch. Sometimes it was just to say hello, but more often it was, "How should I do this?" or, "What would you do in a situation like this?" I was happy to help because they are people I care about, but I also thought it was kind of sad because it shows how important this wisdom and experience is to employees, yet it is not always understood and valued in clear and visible ways inside of organizations.

In most businesses, if you're looking to cut costs or improve the bottom line so you can sell the company, the easiest way to do that is by reducing payroll. And if you're strictly looking at salary, you can probably save five junior people by getting rid of one or two senior-level people. But when you do that, you are robbing the organization—as well as your customers and clients—of some amazing talent and experience at a time when your company needs it the most.

There are plenty of reasons why you should try to keep your valuable employees who are over fifty years old. We've already debunked the myth that older workers don't understand technology, but it bears repeating: we were digital pioneers. We paid three thousand dollars for our first Apple IIs and the first time we lugged that equipment up to the cabin for the weekend we thought about how nice it would be if they made these personal computers more portable. We immediately saw the need for laptops. We also watched the disruption of email, e-commerce, social media, and all the technologies that followed them. Workers over fifty have been through all these changes, and we can help young workers manage the next round of changes, which are inevitable.

EMOTIONAL INTELLIGENCE PAYS OFF

So, older workers get technology, and as I noted earlier, they get Millennials because *they raised them*. But they also bring a wealth of emotional intelligence (EQ) to the job. This is hard to quantify, but it's still a value. If you've managed to stay in your profession until your fifties, then you've probably learned how to let the small things slide, manage conflict, and handle change.

This is not to say that Millennials don't have strong EQs or that all older workers are like Yoda from *Star Wars*. I know plenty of older workers who never developed strong EQs and many millennials who have amazing EQ, but many employers say they value emotional intelligence in their workers above all else, and you can't deny that older workers have had to develop resiliency over the years. They've had to survive change, work through setbacks, deal with terrible clients yelling at them over the phone or survive awful bosses who hurl insults and act like petty children. They've dealt with these things, and they've learned from these experiences. People aren't necessarily born with emotional intelligence. They get it from experience.

ENGAGED AND COMMITTED

The stereotype of the older worker is that they are just playing out the string, collecting a paycheck and waiting around to get the highest possible pension. But the truth is that older workers are much more engaged in their work and their companies than younger workers. They have a much stronger emotional commitment to their work than younger workers, and they are more likely to believe in the company's goals. Older employees aren't merely working for the next paycheck or promotion.

An Aon Hewitt study done for AARP found that workers who are over fifty are the most engaged age group in the workforce.[3] Around 65 percent of those fifty-five and older are engaged while less than 60 percent of younger employees are engaged. That means older workers are much more likely to stay late when they need to (and without being asked), mentor young employees who need it, and do the little things that improve the bottom line. The nonfinancial reasons people stay in their jobs—such as the desire to help coworkers, to remain productive, or simply love of the work—increases with age.

Gallup research confirms that a five-percent increase in engagement brings a three-percent incremental revenue growth. That means a company with $5 billion in revenue could achieve a $150 million revenue boost by having a more engaged workforce. That's significant! It's also conservative: according to Forbes magazine, other studies have found that companies with an engaged workforce see 6 percent higher net profit margins.[4] Another study found that engaged companies have five times higher shareholder returns over five years.

3   https://www.aarp.org/research/topics/economics/info-2015/business-case-older-workers.
    html

4   https://www.forbes.com/sites/kevinkruse/2012/06/22/
    employee-engagement-what-and-why/#62506efd7f37

EMPLOYEE ENGAGEMENT AND MOTIVATION

AGE	ENGAGEMENT	AGE	MOTIVATION
55+	65%	55+	81%
Under 55	58%	Under 55	77%

Source: AARP

Engagement is one reason why older workers help the bottom line, and here's another reason: turnover. Turnover is expensive, and with older workers, you have less of it.

THE HIDDEN COSTS OF HIGH TURNOVER

When you hire someone in their thirties or forties, chances are good that they won't be with you very long. According to AARP, the unexpected or unwanted turnover rate for workers under fifty is 49 percent. For workers over fifty, that rate is less than 30 percent. Here's another way to look at it: the median tenure for a millennial is two years while the median tenure for baby boomers is seven years.

When you factor in how much it costs a company every time an employee leaves and the company has to hire and train a replacement, you start to see why a stable, engaged, and older workforce makes so much sense.

Estimates vary, but one study by the Society of Human Resource Management found that every time a business replaces a salaried employee, it costs from six to nine months of that person's salary.[5] A Center for American Progress looked at the problem according to the type of job and found that the cost of replacing low-paid workers is 16 percent of their annual salary while the cost of replacing a CEO is more than 200 percent of their annual salary.[6]

This is why, as we'll see in the next chapter, some companies like Herman Miller are developing flexible retirement programs that allow them to keep older employees in the workforce longer, so these engaged, savvy older professionals can continue to help the company's bottom line while they help train their replacements. In the next chapter, we'll examine why that makes so much sense.

5   https://www.peoplekeep.com/blog/bid/312123/
     employee-retention-the-real-cost-of-losing-an-employee

6   https://www.americanprogress.org/wp-content/uploads/2012/11/CostofTurnover.pdf

---

CHAPTER SEVEN

GETTING IT RIGHT

LAST YEAR, THE CLOTHING COMPANY CHICO'S came out with a very cool, consumer-facing marketing program with the hashtag #howboldareyou. Women can buy a T-shirt made with their age and the words "years bold". The goal was to empower women not to hide from the number, their age.

It's a cool program, and I ordered three shirts for myself; one for 58, and one for when I turned 59 in September and I'm saving one for my #ImNotDone 60th celebration.

Chico's, which is based in Florida, actually has a *commitment* to hiring older employees. It's part of their business model because it's their target demographic. Most of their executive team are women who are over 50, and many of them over 60. It's good for their business to have older people that manage their store and in higher positions within the corporation.

They actually have challenges sometimes in hiring young people. They would like to, because they believe in the value of a more diverse workplace from an age standpoint, but it can be difficult for them to attract this demographic.

In this chapter, we're going to look at how various workplaces get age inclusivity right. They take responsibility and accept accountability for ageism. They respect older employees, offer programs allow for retirees to transition slowly out of the company, and create apprenticeships across the age groups.

STRATEGIC PLANNING

Herman Miller is a global company based in Zeeland, Michigan that makes high-end office furniture, melding form and function into great concepts for workspaces. They've been around—and thus an employer—for a long time, since 1905, in fact.

I spoke with Tony Cortese, Senior Vice President of People Services (great title, isn't it?), about the company's employee demographic. He said they see it as an important element of strategic planning—not in terms of furniture, but rather their own workforce.

"Like many companies, it became apparent to us that we were pretty rich with boomer-aged employees and that we would come to a time in the next decade when these employees would begin retiring—possibly *en masse*. And the question we asked ourselves was: how do we want to prepare for that?"

They looked at this issue from every level, not just from their perspective as an employer. It wasn't necessarily a concern because it hadn't yet happened, but it was definitely something they wanted to address in a positive manner.

"If an employee walks in and gives you a few weeks' notice on their retirement (which is all we expected them to do) it doesn't give you an awful lot of time to do any strategic planning. It doesn't give you time to figure out what you want to do with the position, like how you want to back-fill it. It doesn't give you time to retain the knowledge of the employee that's leaving, or to find new talent, bring them in, and onboard them."

From the employer's standpoint, it was smart business for them to address this issue upfront. It allowed them to manage the exit strategy of any employee, and it also reduced any anxiety and negative impact the employee might feel knowing this event was on the horizon.

"It was apparent to us that it was equally abrupt for the

employees themselves. When someone gives you two weeks' notice and then commences retirement, for some that can be a rather jarring adjustment and a significant, often startling change."

Tony and his team, along with the full support of Herman Miller management, asked themselves an important question: *What we can do that is beneficial both to the company and to the employee, that would allow for a more planned, deliberate, and people-centered process?*

FLEXIBLE RETIREMENT PROGRAMS

Not many companies do this, with an equal eye to both the employee and the employer. In fact, most don't think about it or do much at all. They would rather hire in a new workforce with new ideas and cheaper pay.

Herman Miller approached it differently. They developed FlexRetirement, a completely voluntary phased retirement program. It's not something they push on their employees; rather the employee is the one who has to initiate the process with their people services consultant and work team leader. The employee has to raise her hand and say she wants it, but very importantly, the company ensures there is no stigma or judgment upon those that choose to opt in.

FlexRetirement basically allows for flexibility for the employees at the end of their career. They can have reduced hours with adjusted pay, which is different than a paid retirement. They can also adjust their time in the office, for instance asking to work 32 hours a week for six months, then scale down to 20 hours a week for the next six. Employees may request to scale back time gradually, or abruptly, however they feel works best for them. The company may not agree, but they do agree to have a conversation that is open to flexibility and finding solutions that benefit both the company and the employee.

As people enter this phase of their career, Herman Miller is also open to exploring project-based work if it fits the employee's needs. The project-based work offers a discreet pass with a concrete beginning, middle, and end. Some companies have found these project positions more suitable and important for an employee at the end of his or her career.

Herman Miller is flexible in general as an employer, but they do have specific requirements for an employee to qualify for the phased retirement program. The employee has to be at least 60 years old with at least five years of employment with the company. Those that qualify can take between six months to two years phasing out of their current role and into retirement.

WATER CARRIERS

This program is another great example for other companies. Herman Miller goes above and beyond when it comes time to celebrate and recognize their more senior, seasoned employees, not just by title, but by experience.

They have a program where, at 20 years of service, employees are asked to join something called the "Water Carrier Group."

There is an ancient tribal belief that the water carriers are the elder people in the tribe who carry the important tribal knowledge. Herman Miller brings that forward to present day. If you have someone who has been at Herman Miller for 20 years, they understand the history of the company. They understand the formal processes of the company, but they *also* understand the informal processes of the company.

Both of these are critical—the informal and formal. This program is the way of recognizing the equal importance of the informal and the formal. The employee manual showcases the set of instructions to be followed, but there is also the informal cultural knowledge that can be shared with new employees by the Water Carriers. They honor these people, and they also hold them accountable: the expectation is that when you become a Water Carrier, you pass on and teach the knowledge you've learned.

Herman Miller has even gone so far as to do research since they instituted their flex retirement program. They've found it to be positively received across the board. It's appreciated by those who participate in the program, by the younger employees who know they might someday take advantage of the program, and by leaders who feel they have more control when it comes to managing the transition when their employees retire.

AFFINITY GROUPS

The company also has an affinity generational-based group. Affinity groups have been around for several decades. They are usually sponsored by a company, complete with an executive sponsor, to demonstrate that various affinities or identities matter and are recognized. There may be a women's group, an LGBT group, or a minority group.

There is currently some very meaningful discussion in business circles as to whether affinity groups help or hurt. If the company is supposed to be inclusive, shouldn't everyone be together? But, for the time being, it's a common practice, if not a best practice! The goal is to enable and empower these groups to discuss certain issues that affect their particular demographic in the workplace. There are not a lot of age-related ones, but Herman Miller has instituted one.

Instead of calling it a "young group" or an "old group," it's just generational. While the company has many millennial employees, the group also has people representing all the age cohorts. People of all ages are there to talk about the issues that they have come across, and how it's relevant across the board. They communicate, work together, and act in ways that demonstrate inclusiveness.

As Tony said, "Quite frankly, like almost anything having to do with inclusiveness and diversity, the best way to break down barriers is through open dialogue and as the executive sponsor of that group, I see it happening with my own eyes every time we get together."

SOMETIMES IT'S JUST GOOD INSTINCTS

While the Herman Miller example is my clear favorite in terms of a purposefully meaningful approach to eradicate ageism in the workplace, sometimes organizations do it right because, well, it's the right thing to do.

One such company was right under my nose. And in full disclosure, I need to add that I serve on their Board of Directors. Old Second Bancorp, is a diversified bank holding company headquartered in Illinois. During one of my monthly Board meetings, we heard from the head of the Bank's Wealth Management department. They had enjoyed a good quarter, in fact a good year, thanks in no small part to one of their best performers, Jackie.

Jackie is 82 years old. I had to talk to her; I was sure I would hear tales of age discrimination along the way. When I asked her my usual "is it a thing" question, she honestly looked a little perplexed. She said, "No, I don't think so, or at least not for me."

I think maybe she thought that wasn't what I was expecting, so she thought more, and then said, "Well actually, yes. I do think I have seen ageism. My boss asks me often if the travel is a problem for me."

That's not ageism, that's compassion. Jackie is still in her job because she is damn good at it. And Old Second has realized that when people entrust their retirement savings to someone, they greatly value the experience that Jackie brings.

While I loved that story, I didn't really think it belonged in the book until someone else from Old Second reached out to me. Damaris runs the very critical function of Customer Service. In her years running the Call Center, she has had three older employees—and I don't mean older as in over-50, I mean older as in over-75! I asked Damaris what managing that demographic was like.

"I'll admit when I first joined as a relatively new people manager, I was slightly intimidated when I learned one of my employees was 78—50 years my senior. What can I possibly teach him?"

In turned out she could teach him plenty. She showed me a note she had saved from him from many years ago where he thanked her for her leadership and all that he had learned from her. As she welled up with tears (he has since passed away), she was very clear that the learning was mutual.

"He has no idea how much I learned about myself and what I was capable of because he as a mature person taught me a great deal about work ethic and commitment."

He also taught her that having a diverse workforce, including older employees, is a good formula, and since Howard, she has also added Joan, who is 83, and Laura, who is 67.

"Sure, sometimes I have to go the extra mile to train them on something new, but they also have a level of patience and manner with customers that the rest of my team constantly learns from."

When I spoke to the bank president about this unusual situation of employing so many older people, his response said it all: "They're good at their job, they want to keep working. Why wouldn't we?"

Why wouldn't we, indeed.

OTHER LEADERS IN AGE INCLUSIVITY

There are several other companies who are handling ageism in a positive and uplifting way.

Barclays, a global bank, expanded its apprenticeship program—basically an internship program—and began actively looking at candidates over the age of 50. They value employees with this life experience and feel that these apprentices will better relate to customers who are seeking loans or looking to invest their wealth with the bank.

They have also employed a team of tech-savvy older employees to help their mature customers with some of their online banking elements. Again, they believe these employees will better relate to their customers and see a bottom-line benefit in investing and seeking out older employees. They document on their website, "Why wouldn't we want to capitalize on the life skills of experienced employees?"

Michelin has a returning retiree employee program that

allows employees to return after a period of time to work with reduced hours. It's a way of recognizing that some people may have retired before they're emotionally or financially ready. They still have important and significant knowledge of the company, so Michelin makes it easy for these retirees to come back to work.

Scripps Health offers generation specific and targeted educational programs. As an example, they have a program that manages the "sandwich generation." This is the generation of people in their late 30s and 40s who have to juggle both the needs of their own children and their aging parents.

GlaxoSmithKline has a formal networking and mentoring program designed to connect older and younger workers while DTE Energy created a network for baby boomers in the workplace.

CVS Caremark offers a snowbird program in which several hundred pharmacists and employees from northern states are transferred each winter to pharmacies in Florida and other warmer states. This works twofold for CVS. It appeals to those older employees who want to head south for the winter, and it also allows CVS to manage the surge in business they need in those areas where their customers flock to the sunshine. The program also establishes an informal mentorship and training for any newly hired employees.

Companies that implement strategies to help older employees—or employees of any age who can benefit of these role models and seasoned professionals—can absolutely see results in employee morale, mentorship programs, and overall success.

_____

CHAPTER EIGHT

10 STEPS TO CREATING CHANGE IN YOUR ORGANIZATION

YOU'VE SEEN HOW OTHERS HAVE ADDRESSED ageism in their companies. Now it's time to embark on the path to create change in your own organization. This shouldn't be daunting or difficult; it requires honest reflection, the commitment to make a shift and the support of a good Human Resources partner. I use the word 'partner' purposefully; I have had the benefit of working with some truly great HR professionals, and I can say with certainty that they have helped me be a better leader and manager. I promise you this: a good HR partner mixed with senior management commitment is one potent combination for the tall task of confronting ageism in the workplace.

For this final chapter, I asked Sarah, a global human resources director for a Fortune 50 company, for specific and actionable strategies you can bring to your own organization.

1. LOOK INWARD AND BE HONEST

The first step is to take a step back, turn around, and really look at the current state of your own organization and assess any ageism that might exist.

As Sarah suggests, "Before you say it doesn't happen here, be honest. Look around. Do a diagnostic audit. I am pretty sure you will be surprised. And not in a good way."

Put your managers to the test. Take a look at your departments and look for discrepancies. Are you hiring a younger demographic, and are you focused on their career development while slowly edging the older employees out the door?

Also assess your customers and your client base. In some cases, younger employees may be a better fit on your sales staff, but in the case of Barclays in the previous chapter, having salespeople who are older may better serve your clientele.

2. CONSIDER THE TRUE COSTS

As I've said consistently throughout this book., you should reduce ageism because it's good for your business. Bring your finance team into the discussion to help you prove it. Along with your HR team, they will be able to assess a true cost/benefit.

It seems logical that you will save money in the short term by replacing a more expensive salary with a less expensive one, but as Sarah has observed, "All too often you typically find out six months later that the younger and cheaper person can only replace *part* of what they did, so you bring in other people to fill in the gaps, and slowly but surely you end up putting costs right back in."

Look at the total financial picture so when you make workforce decisions about your older workers that they are *informed* workforce decisions. Often, you don't actually end up saving money by pushing out older workers.

Throughout my career, when I oversaw reductions, I would bring together my most senior finance officer and most senior HR partner, and together we would look at the long-term financial picture.

3. COMMIT TO VALUING YOUR OLDER EMPLOYEES

This is the time where you commit to truly valuing those

employees who are older. You need to learn about them and understand what matters most—whether it's family, finances, health, or a personal passion.

A 2012 AARP/SHRM study of workers fifty years of age and older found that they stay for several reasons. 78 percent of workers in this group need employment for financial reasons. They need income to live or they need paid benefits, specifically health insurance. 80 percent considered their employer-provided health insurance as a most important consideration for staying in their job.

Only one in five reported working (or looking for work) for non-financial reasons such as enjoyment or fulfillment. But, and this is a key fact, this group did increase with age. Two out of five people surveyed were working for non-financial reasons if they were over the age of 70.

Consistency and familiarity are key to this demographic when it comes to employment. 77 percent planned and hoped to remain in their current job until they retire. Sarah has observed that, not just in the workplace, but in society at large, older workers—even the most confident and self-assured—begin to doubt themselves as they near retirement.

"We go out of our way to make the new hires feel welcomed and valued. Why do we let that slide for our older employees who have often been with us for decades?"

4. PROVIDE FLEXIBILITY

Flexibility is by far the best and most cost-effective tool you have to attract and retain employees *of all ages*. Flexibility can mean a lot of things when it comes to working with older employees and their schedules. Per the AARP/SHRM study, 60 percent of those surveyed were looking for—or were currently working in—a flextime arrangement.

They also wanted employers to consider a formal phased retirement with compressed work schedules and the ability to telecommute as needed.

Other options for flexible schedules can include job-sharing or project-based assignments like at Herman Miller.

As an employer, look at your leave policies. Are they based only on childbearing? Make sure you offer benefits that appeal to older employees, such as paid caregiver leave.

When it comes to exit strategies, consider finding needs in your organization that can serve as "bridge jobs" to allow your older workers to transition into some other kind of work. Expatriate assignments for older workers also make a lot of sense, yet rarely happen, so it's worth exploring within your organization.

5. MAINTAIN AN ENLIGHTENED AND FAIR APPROACH TO TRAINING

Don't let false stereotypes hold you back from investing in employee training and education for your older employees. People of all ages need—and deserve—the opportunity to learn and grow.

Employees of all ages enjoy learning new things, so don't stop setting expectations for employees as they grow older. Encourage niche training or for them to get a certificate or advanced degree. Their insights are equally as valuable, and maybe even more so if they've been within your industry or company for a long period of time. They may have seen an idea cycle through already or know why a specific tool might not work.

Many companies have already discovered to benefits of "reverse mentoring" where a Millennial might help a Boomer understand the business value of new social media platforms. Why not formalize that in your organization to show your commitment to training?

6. DISPLAY VISIBLE SIGNS OF SUPPORT

I'm not just talking AARP posters here. Work to make it visible to everyone that you support the older employees within your organization.

Partner with external support and affiliate groups for older workers. This gets your name out into the public as a place that supports older employees and combats ageism.

Ensure that your recognition program is set up to recognize the mentoring, teaching, and other contributions of your older employees and make that visible to the rest of the organization.

Clearly state in your job notices that mature applicants are welcome, and don't forget to update those marketing materials so you are visibly showcasing workers of all ages.

7. ENSURE YOUR DIVERSITY & INCLUSION STRATEGY REFERENCES AGEISM

If you don't have a Diversity & Inclusion strategy, it's time to make one. This strategy defines your company's mission and practices designed to support a diverse workplace and achieve a competitive business advantage by leverage the effects of diversity.

If you have a D&I strategy already, or once you've drafted one, it's imperative that you review your practices to ensure that they reference ageism. According to PWC's 18th Annual CEO survey, only eight percent of CEO's include age in their D&I strategy.

Some options to consider:

- Consider adding and encouraging employee resource groups that are multi-generational.
- Work through bridging the generation gap and how different generations might learn from one another.
- Implement training for leaders and employees on how to work in a multi-generational workforce. Educate leaders on how to have discussions with late-career/ experienced workers in a way that doesn't put the company at risk and doesn't disengage the worker.

8. ACTIVELY MANAGE THE RETIREMENT TRANSITION

Remember: many of your older workers have lived through more than one recession, so employment pre-dictability and security are of prime importance to them, and they may be quicker to feel anxiety associated with potential staff reductions. Why not ease that anxiety? You can boost employee retention by making it regularly known that you want your older employees to stay and that you remain happy that they continue to work for you.

It's as simple as telling them how much you value them and their presence on the team.

But retirement will come and as we've discussed above, consider offering a phased retirement to your older employees. This may involve them shifting to part-time employment or moving to project-based work, but it's worth exploring options.

Put together a task force with your older employees and ask what they would like to see. Depending on your industry and company, there may be specific flexibility options that do or don't work, but including these employees works to your benefit in multiple ways. They will feel that their input is valuable, they will have ownership in the outcomes, and they will champion the program to other employees. You will also have the opportunity to explore options that you might not have thought of otherwise.

9. MAKE THIS INITIATIVE A PRIORITY

Your senior leadership team and human resources team both need to make the ageism discussion a priority. If HR isn't paying attention, they should be! Chances are that they aren't. According to Society for Human Resource Management (SHRM), less than one-third of HR departments have analyzed the impact of older workers leaving over the next three to five years, and only 17 percent have looked at that over a six- to ten-year horizon.

All companies need to create and enforce hiring and employment policies to reduce ageism. They should ensure that ALL employees—including older ones—have opportunities for training and development. All information should be defined, visible to employees, and clearly stated in the employee handbook and code of conduct.

Sarah explains further, "We need to look beyond avoiding litigation and make sure that we are maximizing talent—ALL talent—for the organization. That means having difficult or awkward conversations. We already ask our leaders to have employee development conversations at a set time every year but are those conversations happening in the same way once an employee hits age 50? I doubt it."

10. HAVE THE CONVERSATION

Have the conversation. The difficult conversation about a planned end to a career almost never happens, but it's time that it starts happening. Today.

Once the conversation has been had, it's important to continue employee development discussions for all employees until their last day of employment. Never make assumptions based on knowledge of personal factors—especially age. Just don't!

Sarah says, "Employees have no incentive to venture there by themselves. If the company doesn't know how (or won't) start the conversation, it can be stressful. Your supervisor may become uncomfortable or won't have a good answer. You may discover the company has no good path. Well, if I'm the employee, I'm just going to shut my mouth and keep my head down for as long as I can. Once you take the genie out of the bottle you can't put it back in!"

Many supervisors don't initiate the conversation because they are afraid it might lead to litigation—or something else unpleasant. While it's an excuse, it's understandable. Take the time to think through how the conversation should go. You don't want to blurt out, "When do you want to retire?" But don't worry about the 20 percent who might not take it well and instead focus on the 80 percent who are anxious to have the conversation.

And the best tip about having the "what's next conversation with someone over 50? Have it with EVERY employee. As Sarah has taught me, a best practice is that you are consistently asking every employee one a year, "How do you want to learn, grow and develop in the next 12 months?" EVERY employee.

If the fear of not having a job or a role for that person is keeping you from having that important conversation that is a lost opportunity for all. Asking the question doesn't mean you have to deliver the solution, but it sure increases the odds that you will have a meaningful and *respectful* discussion about the end of someone's career.

These ten tips are the best way to start creating change in your organization, but it all starts with a genuine commitment to be a truly inclusive employer and don't be hesitant to seek outside help in creating long-lasting change.

AGE INCLUSION BEST PRACTICES

- Compensate fairly. Develop compensation and incentive plans around the goals and objectives of the employees no matter what stage of life they are in. Ensure base pay increases and long-term incentives remain for experienced employees.

- Make inclusion of all generations part of your stated corporate values.

- Rethink processes for high potential identification and development. Employees do not peak at age 50.

Finally, aggressively address weak performers at every age. The last thing you want is a group of 50- and 60-year-olds who have never been told they weren't cutting it! When it comes to professional feedback, level the playing field.

CONCLUSION

I HONESTLY DIDN'T THINK IT WOULD HAPPEN TO me, in spite of everything I knew and saw.

I felt I was at the top of my game and relevant and needed. I worked in a youth-dominated industry surrounded by super-cool, interesting and hip people. The opportunity to listen and observe was endless. I always thought—perhaps too confidently—that I was cool. I didn't have old-fashioned attitudes. I was open to change. Most people seemed to like and respect me, especially younger people. So, in spite of telling myself I would see it coming—I didn't.

Most people who experience ageism don't either. The blow is sudden, swift, and incredibly hurtful. Far too many people told me that the last part of their career was their worst.

Most of us have been taught all our lives that it is impolite to do two things—ask someone how old they are once they hit adulthood, and ask people how much money they make. But I can't help but wonder, if we had asked more of our friends about their salaries, perhaps we would have noticed the inequities between the sexes decades ago. And if we learned that that kick-ass boss or co-worker we love is actually 56, maybe we would lose some of our age bias.

Unfortunately, once you hit 50, there seems to be some sort of "don't ask, don't tell" policy. I remember when I decided to get my first tattoo; it was to honor my 55th birthday. I was proudly showing it to a handful of employees from our (very young) creative group. Word got out, and more and more coworkers came over to see it. Unfortunately, like a game of telephone, the story changed, and the narrative was that it was for my 50th birthday. I had seen enough age bias in my industry, so I let it stand. I shouldn't have. I regret that.

We need to start talking about age. It can't be taboo. The reality is that life trajectory has changed. People are living longer. Anti-aging breakthroughs show we can live to be 120 years old, so why would we stop working half-way through? That only invites boredom and stagnation. We have to face the fact that we're living much longer than previous generations, but we are also healthier. There's no reason not to work and gain an income for much longer, especially if you love what you do. If you retire at age 60, there's a chance you're going to be a burden on someone or run out of money if you live another 20+ years.

Imagine a world where there is no longer a preconceived notion about what age someone becomes irrelevant or undervalued. What if, like every other form of inclusion, you were valued because you were *valuable?* Simply that, nothing more, nothing less?

Imagine a world where nobody feels pressure to leave a company before they are ready to leave, and age is taken off the table as a marker for retirement. What if you put as much thought into the end of your career as you did into the beginning of your career, and it didn't have to be kept a secret until the day you gave notice?

When someone leaves their job in their 50s because there is no place for them, it is really easy to assume that it is a retirement—*early* or otherwise. But even if the person leaves due to their own choice, it's more than likely that they felt unwanted, no longer needed, or suspected their time was limited. That is not how most people want to end their career.

Another way of looking at it is this: *please* do not throw me a surprise retirement party! I'll decide when it's time.

As a country, we're particularly lousy at knowing how to talk about age. We've created a working environment where people are afraid to talk about age, they hide behind HR concerns, and they discount the fact that they are indeed discriminating against older employees.

Older employees offer a wealth of value. They are, quite literally, a *treasure* to any business. They have life experiences and work experiences that can absolutely meld with youth and new ideas and technologies. Imagine a business that leveraged this experience and wisdom, that blended its workforce into a truly diverse, agile, intelligent, cohesive, and *kind* organization. Imagine how unstoppable that business would be.

It's time to talk about ageism in the workplace. A change is coming, and it starts here. Today. With you.

ABOUT THE AUTHOR

PATTI TEMPLE ROCKS has spent her entire four-decade career in the communications industry. She has been in senior roles with leading global agencies, both PR and advertising, and worked with blue chip clients from the worlds of Consumer Goods, Healthcare, B2B, Financial Services and Quick Service Restaurants. She has also *been* a client, as the head of Public Affairs and Reputation for a Fortune 50 company, where she was recognized as Marketer of the Year for three years in a row by B2B Magazine and won numerous awards for a multidisciplinary campaign she brought to the company.

She has launched new products and renewed passion around old products; built brands and protected and repaired brands; navigated through crises, and averted even more. She has counseled executive leadership teams and been part of them. She has been both an agent of change and a steady guide throughout the process.

Among all her professional accomplishments and accolades, the one that matters most to Patti is being known as an inspirational leader who is still connected to the hundreds of people she has had the privilege to manage.

Patti serves on the Board of Directors for a regional bank and is currently consulting with businesses on Communications Strategy. She speaks on topics including Authentic Leadership, Managing Change, Agency/Client Relationships, and of course, Ageism in the Workplace.

She lives in Chicago with her husband Bob and their two golden retrievers. She has a son in college and two adult step children.

To learn more about this issue and get in touch with Patti, visit her website, http://imnotdone.rocks.

Made in the USA
Coppell, TX
08 January 2020

14240054R00104